OUT WITH THE TIDE

BLACK YEOMANRY

LIFE ON ST. HELENA ISLAND

BY

T. J. WOOFTER, JR.

OCTAGON BOOKS

A DIVISION OF FARRAR, STRAUS AND GIROUX

New York   1978

Copyright, 1930, by Henry Holt and Company, Inc.
Copyright renewed © 1958 by T. J. Woofter, Jr.

*Reprinted 1978
by special arrangement with Holt, Rinehart and Winston, Inc.*

OCTAGON BOOKS
A DIVISION OF FARRAR, STRAUS & GIROUX, INC.
19 Union Square West
New York, N.Y. 10003

Library of Congress Cataloging in Publication Data

Woofter, Thomas Jackson, 1893-
    Black yeomanry.

    Reprint of the ed. published by H. Holt, New York.
    1. St. Helena Island, S.C. 2. Afro-Americans—South Carolina—St. Helena Island. I. Title.
F277.B3W9   1978   975.7′99   78-938
ISBN 0-374-98744-0

Manufactured by Braun-Brumfield, Inc.
Ann Arbor, Michigan
Printed in the United States of America

To
ROSSA B. COOLEY
AND
GRACE B. HOUSE

WHOSE DEVOTION TO THE REALITIES OF EDUCATION HAS GIVEN VITAL LEADERSHIP TO ST. HELENA AND ITS PEOPLE

PREFACE

The land and people of St. Helena Island are the same which lend charm to the work of Julia Peterkin and of DuBose Heyward; and they have that social significance which leads the student of human culture into all possible by-ways of scientific inquiry. The plot of this volume is the life and development of the St. Helena community, rather than the life of individuals. It is life at a stage somewhat more advanced than that of *Black April* and *Porgy* because the people of St. Helena have had more advantages; and its description is more unified than the fragmentary studies of folk culture of the older type.

It would be impossible to describe the Island adequately without including the picturesque elements, but the chief objective of this work has not been the picturesque, in the sense that it may properly concern the littérateur. Complete and logical description of those customs and conditions which have made the community what it is today has been the primary aim, with picturesqueness a secondary consideration. A more rounded and detailed picturization of the life of the whole people has been substituted for the characterization and plot of semi-fiction.

Such portraiture has its human interest and scientific values, but in the light of the present widespread desire to improve race relations it has its practical applications also. In assembling this material practical questions often influenced its arrangement. What are the effects of land ownership upon the Negro? To what extent and under what conditions does he show improvability in health, in family life and morals, in scientific methods of agriculture? What are the results of the practical type of education, pioneered by Hampton and Tuskegee? Of what value to the Negro community are such agencies as the Rosenwald Schools, Supervising Teachers, Rural Nurses, Farm Demonstration Agents, Home Demonstration Agents? Information of value in answering these questions is gathered by observing a Negro group isolated from other influences, but served by these constructive programs.

Some objections were raised to studying St. Helena on the ground that this Island is not typical of general Negro conditions. This we felt was an asset rather than a liability; first, because there is enough of basic similarity between this and other Negro communities to make many of the observations on this Island of significance to the rural Negro in general; and second, because many of the constructive forces which have made St. Helena exceptional are those which need most to be described and analyzed.

Back of the statements made in this summary is the work of a number of specialists in different fields of social science who spent varying periods on the Island, studying their particular phase of its life. Much of the detail of their work will be published in other books and articles giving the items wanted for special reference. The statistical detail has been included in the appendix of this volume.

Chapter II gives the gist of the valuable historical documents, among which many were original plantation records found by Dr. Guion Griffis Johnson.

PREFACE vii

Chapter III is the summary of a very interesting and detailed study made by Dr. Guy B. Johnson of the rich island folklore and folk songs. These materials will be treated in a separate volume on History and Folk Backgrounds. The statement on population and migration was worked out with the advice of Dr. Frank A. Ross and the collaboration of Mr. Clyde V. Kiser, who is preparing a fuller factual statement on the migration of the Islanders and their adaptation to city life. Dr. Joseph Peterson of Peabody College and Dr. E. A. Hooton of Harvard directed students who made psychological tests and physical measurements on the Island, and the details of their findings will be available later.

On the economic life of the Island valuable advice was secured from Mr. O. M. Johnson of the U. S. Department of Agriculture and Dr. W. H. Mills of Clemson College. The chapter on Taxation represents the investigation of Dr. Clarence Heer of the University of North Carolina, and the observations on crime contained in the chapter on Religion are those of Dr. Roy M. Brown of the same university. In presenting the material on family life, the collaboration of Dr. Ernest R. Groves was helpful. The statistical and clerical work has been efficiently handled by Miss Jessie Alverson.

In addition to the specialists, we wish particularly to acknowledge indebtedness for the cooperation of the Principals of Penn School and their whole staff of teachers and community workers, without whom such an intimate contact with the community would have not been possible.

The means of assembling this group of students and concentrating their thought on the effort to present a rounded picture of the development of this community were provided by the Social Science Research Council and the Institute for Research in Social Science at the University of North Carolina. The Council granted to the University a fund to supplement the regular budget of the Institute for Research in Social Science, thereby making it possible for the work to be done.

In the preparation of the manuscript the workers were inspired to especial effort by the gracious offer of the Yaddo Corporation, allowing the use of Triuna Island during the summer of 1929 for writing and conferences.

Triuna Island on
Lake George, New York,
September, 1929.

CONTENTS

I. THE SEA ISLANDS 3
    The way to St. Helena. Isolation. The decay of plantations. Negro yeomen. The kindly people. Their heritage. The developing forces, national and international interest in St. Helena.

II. COTTON AND CONTRABANDS by GUION GRIFFIS JOHNSON 13
    The English come. Staple crops. The management of slaves. Freedom. Land-buying. Early struggles.

III. ST. HELENA SONGS AND STORIES by GUY B. JOHNSON 48
    The dialect of Old England. The songs of early America. The stories and superstitions of Africa.

IV. THE PEOPLE 82
    Increase. Movement. Effects of the movement. The old widows. Islanders in the city.

V. HEALTH 103
    A good place to die of old age. From superstition to medicine. No indigenous tuberculosis. Remarkably low infant death rate. Midwives and birthing.

VI. BREADWINNING 114
    Dividing time between farming, fishing and oyster factories. Incomes. How $420 becomes a competence. Household aid from the home demonstration agent.

VII. AGRICULTURE 132
    The farm tradition. Complications in land ownership. Hard work. Cotton, corn, potatoes and

CONTENTS

peanuts. Fighting the boll weevil. Oxen and poultry. South Carolina's first cooperative. Farm relief from Penn School and the demonstration agent.

VIII. TAXATION AND GOVERNMENT BENEFITS *by* CLARENCE HEER 158
The burden. The benefits. Roads and Schools.

IX. EDUCATION 186
Yearning to learn. Inadequate public schools. Poorly paid teachers. Excellent private instruction. Education permeating the life of a community. Authority in the community.

X. THE HOME 205
Mating. The slave family. Illegitimacy. Old widows and "adopteds." The home. Pride of ownership. National prizes for "better homes."

XI. PLAY 219
Play and worship. The shout. Children's games. Holidays. Penn School program.

XII. RELIGION 225
"Seeking." Ceremonies and services. All Baptists. Praise houses. Crime kept at a minimum by churches.

XIII. THE WORTH OF EXPERIMENT 243
Experiment of building a Negro community started and abandoned by Federal Government. Local government not effective. Private philanthropy has carried on. Some results in improving Negro life. Applicability to other Southern areas. World-wide significance in dealing with backward races.

APPENDICES 256
How we got acquainted. Statistical Information. Appendix to Chapter IX.

ILLUSTRATIONS

OUT WITH THE TIDE	*Frontispiece*
	FACING PAGE
HALE AT EIGHTY-EIGHT	12
COFFIN PLANTATION	46
SCREENED WITH FIGS AND POMEGRANATES	46
A BETTER HOME	108
MIDWIVES' CLASS	108
CANNING EXHIBIT	128
DOMESTIC SCIENCE	128
COTTON	144
SUGAR CANE	144
TILLING	158
POUNDING RICE	158
ROSENWALD SCHOOL	190
SCHOOL GARDENING	190
PUBLIC SCHOOL, EXTERIOR AND INTERIOR	204
COMMUNITY HOUSE	222
BAPTIZING	240
ANTE-BELLUM EPISCOPAL CHURCH	254
AN ISLAND GRAVE	254

BLACK YEOMANRY
LIFE ON ST. HELENA ISLAND

CHAPTER I

THE SEA ISLANDS

We are climbing Jacob's ladder,
We are climbing Jacob's ladder,
We are climbing Jacob's ladder,
Soldier of the cross.

Every round goes higher and higher,
Soldier of the cross.

Sinner, do you love my Jesus?
Soldier of the cross.

If you love Him, why not serve Him?
Soldier of the cross.

Do you think I'd make a soldier?
Soldier of the cross.

We are climbing higher and higher,
We are climbing higher and higher,
We are climbing higher and higher,
Soldier of the cross.

We move along stretches of shady road where detours and concrete alternate on the new coastal highway. It is spring and jessamine festoons the trees. Cardinals, not singly but in flocks, make scarlet streaks as they rise from the roadway ahead. Occasionally a gay-colored but shy nonpareil darts into the protecting brush of the fields, and fat quail hurry across the track. Swamps and woodland alternate with level black fields where the plow turns the sandy loam for a new crop. Nature is prodigal in the Sea Islands.

This stretch of highway from Charleston to Savannah cuts the center of the Sea Island area. Formerly the seat of some of the South's proudest and richest plantations, it now has only memories of its past glories. A few of the once gay mansions stand in faded grandeur at the head of wide avenues of aged moss-hung oaks. Many have passed into the hands of the outlander as hunting preserves. Still others are truck farms with an oak-bordered driveway leading to ruins. The bulk of the land is in woods or fallow fields. Scattered along the highway and tucked away on side roads are many small farms of Negroes who have been freeholders since emancipation.

Nature and man have conspired to strip the South Carolina tidewater of its glories. First naval stores and timber brought wealth and were exhausted. Next indigo, rice, and cotton flourished. The fresh water areas along the swamps and rivers teemed with the laborers on the rice plantations. The owners had their own schooners and loaded their product at the plantation wharf for European market. They were as familiar with London as with New York. But indigo became unprofitable when the bounty was removed and rice was eventually produced at prices below those profitable to the South Carolina planter. Now as the causeways cross the marshes one sees only rotting flood gates and choked ditches. For many years nature granted to the sea coast a monopoly on silky cotton of superior staple known the world over as "sea island." Prosperity again smiled. In the meantime phosphate mining throve and declined when cheaper phosphates were discovered elsewhere. Nature again brought disaster in the shape of a bug—the weevil—which definitely ruined sea island cotton production.

Through all these reverses many of the proud plantations were gradually abandoned or sold off in small tracts to Negro farmers who have held on to their humble homes. On St. Helena, our destination, the transition from white to Negro ownership was sudden, dramatic and almost complete as far as resident owners are concerned. Lands of owners absent with Confederate armies were sold for taxes and an old, established civilization was replaced by an experiment.

Through the changes of two centuries a definite culture has developed in the region. Its characteristics were fixed by the large plantation where great masses of black people worked with the minimum contact with whites. It was preserved by isolation after the planters moved away.

The coastal highway branches and we follow the side road fifteen miles to Beaufort. There we look across the Beaufort River to St. Helena and Ladies Islands. They are the seaward township of Beaufort County. Beyond is the Atlantic. In ante-bellum days the journey which we are making from Charleston to Beaufort required three days of alternating boat and carriage travel. We make it on the new highway in something over three hours. Even after railways were built the journey to Beaufort was round about and the final stage of reaching St. Helena was accomplished by a casual ferry across the Beaufort River. Thus, of the isolated sea coast country, St. Helena has been the most isolated, thickly populated Island.

Shut off from the channels of world intercourse, the

forces moulding life here have been more evident than those moulding communities less isolated. In other communities the people have been more in contact with outsiders. Here land and home ownership, education, and a strong religious institution have been at work. We had always felt, since first seeing the place, that this Island was a test tube for the observation of the action of constructive forces on an isolated Negro group of as pure African descent as could be found in the country.

As we approached in 1927, we saw the new highway smoothing the way into Beaufort. More revolutionary still, a new bridge was pushing its way across the Beaufort River. The last barrier of isolation was being removed. If the unique character of the place was to be captured it must be done quickly before the passage back and forth blended St. Helena culture too strongly with that of the mainland. So a few months later, arrangements all made, we returned to live awhile among these most kindly people and to endeavor to picture their life in all its ramifications.

As soon as we reach its shores we feel the difference. Here the houses are not grouped as in the tenant quarters on the inland plantations and in the old "nigger house yards." Nor are they widely scattered. They are sprinkled thickly along the cart tracks and stand in the midst of the ten- and twenty-acre farms, within hailing distance of one another and of the road. The neat story and a half dwellings are embellished with small porches and bay windows. The light blue and green paint on the doors and shutters is gay. Flower yards, with luxurious fig and pomegranate bushes, make a screen of shy retirement.

Pride of ownership shows in paint and orderliness, a contrast to the drab tenant houses of the interior.

The road is rough and the ruts wind as they follow the erratic course of the plodding oxen. The high land is frequently indented with gleaming tidal inlets where crabs scuttle and where low water uncovers beds of oysters on the bordering mud flats. Thus St. Helena is fringed with peninsulas and smaller islands surrounded at low tide by a broad grassy marsh.

At our house we meet Uncle Sam, eighty-eight, tall, sprightly, shrewd, and kindly. He has known slavery, war, and freedom. Though he is our caretaker and "raises de fire," he still owns his fifteen acres and house "down de road," and "meks de crop" regularly.

His sister, Aunt Rose, is waiting with a typically African greeting, a present of eggs. We must be made to feel at home. Beside her, grinning a welcome, are four " 'dopteds" of varying age ready to sing us a spiritual or tell us a wonderful animal story—one which Uncle Remus overlooked.

They all meet us with outstretched hand. "Please to meet your acquaintance," says Uncle Sam, without any of that embarrassment found among Negroes who have had the color line constantly emphasized in meeting white people. So few white people have lived here that the attitude toward us is not strained. We feel just like a friend, not like a person separated by the barrier of race. Throughout we find that our converse with the Islanders is franker and less embarrassed than with Negroes who have had the badges of racial difference emphasized daily.

They have not been trained to expect frequent rebuffs from white people. We are cordially invited to weddings, funerals, and praise services; to participate in church collections and to join the shouting-ring. We were drawn closely into community affairs.

Officially welcomed, we become residents of Tom Fripp Plantation. Within the Island there is a definite persistence of the old plantation boundaries as local geographic divisions. Although the ante-bellum plantations have long ceased to be units of ownership, they still constitute units of local community division. Each plantation has a local pride and the rudiments of a community organization. In describing their place of residence the inhabitants do not say St. Helena Island but "Tom Fripp Plantation." Leadership is not Island-wide but distributed among the "old folks" of different plantations. In this sense the whole Island is not a community but a series of communities which have evolved from ante-bellum plantations. Some of these units have shrunk until they are rather small to be considered as communities and yet there is seemingly no tendency to coalesce with large units.

In government, Ladies and St. Helena Islands form a township of Beaufort County. It is soon evident, however, that local government has had little enough to do with the development of the people. Beyond the most elementary provisions for keeping order and building roads and schools, the Islanders have been left to themselves. The Negroes are not voters and there are no more than twenty qualified white voters. Politically, we have come to one of the many rotten boroughs of the South, which are taxed

THE SEA ISLANDS

as the powers that be see fit, and benefited by government only as the same powers choose.

Even in such a simple and homogeneous settlement the search for the forces which have made Uncle Sam and Aunt Rose what they are, and which will shape their " 'dopteds" in the future, will take us far afield. Many bits of varied types of information will have to be assembled and evaluated.

Africa is here. Physical traits, and doubtless many subtler cultural traits, are African. Down the road from the house goes a straight-backed girl balancing a bucket of water on her head with a natural grace possible only to Africans. Here stands Aunt Rose with her present of eggs, welcoming us exactly as we would be welcomed in Nigeria. The continent of mystery is woven through the folklore and superstition and throbs in the periodic shouts of the praise houses. These, however, are incidental. There is astonishingly little from Africa which is of functional importance in the present day activities of this isolated Negro culture.

Old England and early America are here in the songs and the dialect which fall so strangely on the ear, in the ox-drawn, two-wheeled carts which we so frequently pass, in the yeoman culture of small plots of land with its independent life not fashioned after a money economy. Long arms of the past reach down through tradition to shape the life of the people today.

But the more immediate past is influential also. Uncle Sam's praise house, of which he is the leader, is a peculiar religious institution, a plantation branch of the church. It originated in plantation days when religious services for slaves were held on plantations rather than in churches. Its hymns are reminiscent of early American revivals. It controls local disputes, as the early churches did, with the result that "lawing" on the Island is at a minimum. Those who claim that the Negro is inherently criminal are confronted with an area extraordinarily free from crime.

Landownership—that most powerful factor differentiating these farmers from the farm tenants of the interior black belt—came in reconstruction days. This was the first Confederate territory with a plantation organization to be taken over by the Union armies. Here the hopes of "forty acres and a mule" were born, and the government's initial policies of dealing with freedmen were worked out. Lincoln was fully conversant with Civil War happenings on St. Helena, and his thinking on the difficult politics of dealing with freedmen was being shaped by these events. Here the early experiences in Negro education were encountered, and mission societies began to make educational programs.

More interesting are the contemporary forces at work in this isolated community. Their results can be traced more clearly here because of the isolation. Here are people with a purer African tradition and blood than other Negro groups in the United States. Physical isolation has tended to strengthen tradition, but cultural contact with contemporary movements has been supplied by Penn School, which has brought to them the riches of ideas.

This school was the first Southern Negro school to be opened. Its staff includes one of the first and most efficient Negro public health nurses. It has sponsored the first agricultural cooperative enterprise, either for white or

THE SEA ISLANDS 11

colored, in South Carolina. It has brought to the people the constructive influences of the farm demonstration agent, home demonstration agent, and nurse. Education on such a broad community scale, applied to people whose other contacts with white culture have been limited, gives us a supreme test of the adaptability of the Negro. What has been accomplished under these circumstances on St. Helena is of vital significance in exemplifying what might be accomplished in other areas of the South. In a study of the activities and accomplishments of these agencies much light is thrown on the practical aspects of race betterment.

Here the infant death rate has been reduced so low as to indicate an astonishing improvement in the fundamentals of life. Homes have been expanded and improved, not only by renovating the house but also by stimulating pride in the household. Farming has been diversified and better methods of tillage demonstrated. The record of how this was done is an open book before us in the experience of St. Helena.

We soon learn, however, that Uncle Sam has brothers and Aunt Rose has children in the outside world. Not all the Islanders remain at home. The community educational program has been sufficient to palliate but not to reverse the sweeping economic forces which have depressed agriculture throughout the United States, and especially in the boll weevil area. St. Helena has therefore sent sons and daughters far and wide. This exodus emphasizes the interest of the whole United States in the happenings in Southern rural areas. Country boys, white and colored, move from them into the cities and their contribution to the city depends upon whether they have been well or ill prepared back home for life's emergencies. In an even broader sense we are impressed that the significance of experiences on St. Helena is world-wide. Uncle Sam has been interviewed by African missionaries and government officials. At Penn School Miss Cooley keeps a map of Africa studded with a growing number of colored tacks each representing a missionary or educational official who has visited the Island and the school to make practical observations on their successful educational program. Funds have been provided for the development of four institutions modeled after Penn School in South Africa. The constructive experience of the South during the past sixty years, as it is epitomized on the Island, is of world-wide significance. All over the globe people of western culture are endeavoring to deal with peoples of other cultures. Wherever they are concerned with the human values in the subject people rather than with exploitation, they are beginning to feel that the trial and error experiences of America in advancing the Negro along fundamental and practical lines have a value in pointing the way to the adjustment of other diverse racial elements.

HALE AT EIGHTY-EIGHT

CHAPTER II

COTTON AND "CONTRABANDS" [1]

Go down, Moses,
Way down in Egypt land,
Tell old Pharaoh:
"Let my people go."

"Gun-shoot!" There was no need, on the morning of November 7, 1861, for the excited slaves to pass the word around. They could hear for themselves the dull explosions on Port Royal Sound rolling across the water and echoing up the tidal creeks. No work in the fields today! All the hands felt the tingle of great events in the air. They were gathered near "de big house" receiving swift orders of an unusual nature.

Limus, the driver, was consulting importantly with the master. Ned, the carpenter, was feverishly putting some last-minute repairs on the boat, spurred on by impatient commands from the overseer.

"Limus, Ned has finished. Get ten good oarsmen to launch the boat and take the Mistress to Walterboro."

Limus turned to the chattering group. "Yunna jump. Massa want ten men to pit de boat een de creek." The ten oarsmen jumped.

---

[1] This chapter is a summary of a more detailed presentation of history which will be published separately. Documentary references are, therefore, omitted.

"Four more to take the Mistress's things"; and the four were chosen.

The mistress rushed up. "Isn't there any more time? There are so many things—"

"No, we cannot take any chances. You must hurry. The boat is launched and the oarsmen ready. You will be in Walterboro with Cousin Sally by night."

"But, John,—the cotton."

"It will be burned if necessary. It must never fall into Yankee hands."

"Do Jedus," groaned Limus, "hun'erd fifty bales dis year. Nigh all prime cotton."

But the cotton was never burned. That had been postponed too long. The master had been confident, as had the other St. Helena planters, that the Federal fleet, which had been assembling off Hilton Head for three days, was gathering to attack Charleston. What could they want with Beaufort and the Sea Islands? Fort Beauregard and Fort Walker had only thirty-nine guns in their feeble batteries while the Confederate scouts reported that the flag-ship, alone, of the Federal "armada" mounted sixty.

It was too late now to destroy the scattered cotton. That should have been done two days ago. Even as the mistress left, the attacking fleet, in battle array, was forcing its way past the puny fire of the Confederate forts and turning to pour volleys into their front and flank.

A message arrived from Captain Fripp of the St. Helena Mounted Riflemen. "Prepare all transportation to aid in the evacuation of troops and report to the company immediately." What irony! For weeks the Riflemen had been planning the strategy of meeting the invader, and now

COTTON AND "CONTRABANDS" 15

there was nothing to do in face of overwhelming numbers but prepare a hasty and undignified retreat.

Well, orders were orders. "Limus, hitch up all carts, man the bateaux and scows, and saddle Vixen."

"I am going for a while. Get as much cotton picked out as you can and I will bring you something when I come back."

So it was that the master looked for the last time upon his house.

When he had left there was much babble but no disorder. "Buh Limus," said one, "is dem nyankees coming hyar?"

"I do' know."

"What dey duh do w'en dey come?"

"De vhite man do w'at he please wit' us. We be dere niggers if dey come."

"Do Jedus, Buh Limus! I hyar nyoung Massa Pope say dem nyankees be pure debbil and dey sell us to Cuba."

"Doan' crack your teeth again, Nigger. Nyankees lub cotton jus' like Carolina buckra. You hear de massa. Git een de fiel'." [2]

It was so that the conquering troops found them—still under the sway of the driver; still getting out the valuable cotton. "The effect of the victory," wrote General W. T. Sherman, in charge of the Expeditionary Corps, "is startling. Every white inhabitant has left the island. The wealthy islands of St. Helena and Ladies, and most of Port Royal are abandoned by the whites, and the beautiful estates of the planters, with all their immense property,

[2] These quotations are not exact but follow closely accounts of happenings on St. Helena on this date.

left to the pillage of the hordes of apparently disaffected blacks."

The capture of St. Helena by the Federal forces marked the beginning of its development as a Negro community. Before 1861 there had been a century and a half of uninterrupted development of plantations and before that nearly two centuries of alternate occupation for short periods by Indians, Spanish, French, and English.

In 1521 Quexos reconnoitered the South Atlantic seaboard for Spain and in 1525 he named the eastern projection of St. Helena Island *Punta de Santa Elena* in honor of his patron, and thus gave the name which the English later applied to a sound, an island, and a parish. Although Spain claimed Santa Elena as the northernmost frontier of its dominion in the new world, it made no effort to establish a mission there until Jean Ribaut had built Charlesfort in 1562 on Parris Island, adjacent to St. Helena, and claimed for France the first Protestant settlement in North America. Menendez, adelantado and captain-general of Florida, destroyed the French fort four years later and erected the presidio San Filipe near its site. The Catholic fathers at once began their ministrations to the Indians under the protection of a garrison, but after ten years the Indians turned upon their teachers and burned the fort.

In 1577 the Spanish erected Fort San Marcos, a more substantial building, and stoutly defended Santa Elena against English encroachment for forty years after that country first turned covetous eyes upon the region. In 1685 Spain wiped out Lord Cardross' settlement at Port

Royal, as the English called the Santa Elena region, and they did not actually concede the territory to Great Britain until 1763.

English planters in the West Indies had, for several years, been longing for new land when they sent Captain William Hilton, in 1663, to explore the South Carolina coast. In the same year eight English noblemen, including Sir John Colleton, a Barbadian planter, obtained a patent, as Lords Proprietors, for the region including Spanish Santa Elena and six years later sent out three vessels with instructions to settle there. The Spanish threat and the hostility of the Indians were sufficient to frighten the colonists away and they founded Charles Town instead.

These early settlers were eager for "the principal place in Carolina, call'd Port-Royal" to be "seated with English and Scots in considerable number, because 't is a bold Port, and also a Frontier upon the Spaniard at Augustine," but it was not until after 1690 that the Lords Proprietors granted the first warrant for land near St. Helena Island. Beginning with the patent to Thomas Nairne, an Indian trader, the Proprietors, by 1711, had issued twenty-five warrants for more than eleven thousand acres of land on the Island itself. In 1715 the Yamasee Indians suddenly opened war upon the little band of colonists and had slain 200 of them before the massacre could be stopped. But the provincial officials turned disaster into victory by expelling the Yamasees from South Carolina and opening their lands for settlement.

The applications for grants came more frequently after the Yamasee War, but at best the settlement about St.

Helena grew slowly. As late as 1730 the population of the parish was not more than seventy families. Various acts passed by the provincial assembly indicate that the town of Beaufort was small and its commerce unimportant even to the time of the Revolution.

These early invaders of a doubtful frontier were adventurers from many sections. They came, as the records of St. Helena's Parish show, from Barbados, Bermuda, Bridgenorth and Ludlow in Shropshire, Bristol, Canterbury in Kent, Dorchester, Liverpool, London, Ireland, Scotland, Wales, Switzerland, and France. There were among them, according to the parish register: barbers, carpenters, coopers, cordwainers, traders, leather dressers and breeches makers, laborers, mariners, masters of piraguas, merchants, overseers, painters, planters, pump makers, sailors, schoolmasters, shipwrights, shoemakers, soldiers, surgeons, tailors, and weavers. Seasoned planters came from Barbados, merchants from England, adventuresome tradesmen and indentured white servants with scarcely enough to pay their passage money from many places.

The Lords Proprietors had hoped to attract to their province chiefly the prosperous planters from the West Indies so that the plantation régime already well established there might be quickly set up in the new country. Accordingly, Lord Ashely wrote to Sir John Yeamans in 1670:

> I am glad to heare soe many considerable men come from ye Barbados for wee finde by deare experience y^t noe other are able to make a Plantacon but such as are in condition to stock & furnish themselves ye rest serve only to fill up numbers & live upon us & therefor now we have a competent number untill we are

better stocked with provisions I am not very fond of more company unless they be substantial men.

Although many who later became prominent planters in South Carolina first started their fortunes in the new world as merchants and traders, experienced planters from other colonies pointed the way for them by the introduction of the slave system which was to distinguish the South Carolina lowlands for the next century and a half.

These early planters, contrary to the instructions of the Lords Proprietors, did not give their attention to the cultivation of semi-tropical plants, such as indigo, cotton, and ginger, which could not be raised in England and therefore had a ready market there. Instead they turned to that which was nearest at hand, the exploitation of the natural resources of the land. They cultivated some maize and a few other food crops, but the most of their time went to hewing timber and preparing "Tarr made of the resinous juice of the pine (which boyl'd to a thicker consistence is pitch)."

The site of the town of Kingstree, north of Charleston, was granted with the reservation that a certain giant pine be held for a mast for one of his Majesty's vessels, and the great live oaks of the coast furnished stout ribs for colonial vessels as well as for those of the mother country. The framework of *Old Ironsides* was hewed from the live oaks of St. Simon's Island.

Although some indigo had been grown in the province from the first, it was not until 1744 that it became a staple crop in South Carolina, gradually supplementing naval stores as an export. Five years later Parliament allowed a bounty of six pence a pound on indigo, and production of the dye leaped ahead. On the eve of the Revolution Charles Town was exporting more than a million and a half pounds.

The light, dry soil in St. Helena's Parish was especially adapted to the cultivation of indigo and the dye produced there always commanded the top price in market. It was a crop, too, which fitted in easily with the manufacture of naval stores. It took the place on the Sea Islands of the cultivation of rice which was grown extensively on the fresh water ponds and rivers fringing the coast. Even after the Revolution cut off the bounty on indigo, the plant was cultivated until St. Helena planters found a new and more profitable staple to take its place.

Soon after the Revolution several Georgia planters experimented with the growth of a long-fiber cotton which they had obtained from the Bahama Islands. To their gratified surprise the seed produced a finer cotton than that grown in the Bahamas, and the fiber brought a high price in market. The culture soon spread into South Carolina where the first successful crop was raised on Hilton Head in the vicinity of St. Helena Island.

Prices rose from nine pence a pound in the early days of the production to as high, in 1828, as two dollars for the finest quality, and dropped again in the last half of the ante-bellum period until planters received sixty-two cents and even as low as twenty-one cents for prime cotton. While, as with all crops, the less capable planters were unsuccessful, rich rewards went to the intelligent and industrious. Especially in the early days of the cultivation of

COTTON AND "CONTRABANDS"

sea island cotton, it was not uncommon for a planter to make his fortune in a few years. Peter Gaillard, of St. John's, Berkely, made an average of $340 a hand, and William Brisbane, of St. Paul's, was so wealthy after two years of growing sea island cotton that he retired and sold his plantation to William Seabrook at an exorbitant price, but Seabrook paid for it in two years.

As soil and climate conspired to give the southern sea coast a monopoly of this choice crop, it quickly supplanted the cultivation of indigo and became the dominant factor in shaping the economic and social development of the region. The ante-bellum sea island cotton area, of which St. Helena was roughly the center, was a belt of the coast from twenty to thirty miles wide, extending from the Santee River on the north to the Florida Everglades, where cotton controlled the life, not only of the ante-bellum planters and their slaves, but also the life of the freedmen from the Civil War until the advent of the boll weevil in 1918.

In the development of the plantation economy, the settlers of South Carolina soon found, as those in the West Indies had at an earlier date, that the sparsely settled province could not meet their labor needs. The climate, too, was injurious to the health of white people during the summer. Encouraged by the Lords Proprietors, they turned at once to the African slave market. The slaves soon outnumbered the whites in the province, and this predominance of blacks continued in South Carolina until 1920.

While a few planters brought their slaves with them from the West Indies, by far the greatest number stocked their plantations from the Charleston slave market. Just as the planters themselves came from many different places in the old and new worlds, so did the slaves come from many different tribes and localities in Africa. Gambia and Guiney Negroes were the favorite slaves, but the Charleston market also advertised "Calabars from Bight," Coromantines, "healthy young Fantees" and cargoes from "the Masse-Congo country," "Cape Mount on the Grain Coast," "Bassa on the Winward Coast," Bance Island, Angola.

Although merchants, in selling newly imported Negroes, invariably advertised the tribe or geographic section from which the Negroes came, it is interesting that none of these facts were mentioned in selling seasoned slaves. It would seem that tribal differences tended to disappear as the slave became seasoned. The evidence concerning the slave trade indicates, therefore, that the Negro people of the Sea Islands, the so-called Gullah Negroes, were not originally a homogeneous group and that their distinguishing characteristics are those of culture and not of blood.

In 1791 a St. Helena planter's wife declared that the chief interest of the Islanders was in accumulating a large slaveholding. The profits of their crops, she wrote, are "mostly expended in the purchase of Negroes, & nothing is so much coveted as the pleasure of possessing many slaves.—These singularities are inherited from their Fore-Fathers—& many follow so closely in the path thru which their Ancestors trod as to deny themselves the Comforts & conveniences of life."

At the beginning of the ante-bellum period the sea island plantations had become fairly well stocked and from then

COTTON AND "CONTRABANDS" 23

on natural increase ordinarily supplied the demand for slaves. In 1790 there were in Beaufort District, of which St. Helena Island was a part, 585 slaveholders with an average of twenty-four slaves each. Seventy years later the number of slaveholders had almost doubled and the average had risen to thirty each. At this time, 1860, 60 per cent of the owners held less than twenty slaves each, but the remaining 40 per cent held 85 per cent of the total number of slaves in the district. These averages for Beaufort District were twice as large as the average for the state as a whole.

On St. Helena Island the holdings were even larger than the average for the district. In 1850 there were only 112 white males to 3,581 slaves in the parish, which included, besides St. Helena Island, Ladies Island, and a part of Port Royal Island. Edward L. Pierce, agent for the Government, reported that there was an average of about fifty-two slaves to the plantation on St. Helena at the beginning of the Civil War. He found on one plantation as many as two hundred slaves; on two others, more than a hundred and on the remainder from thirty-eight to eighty.

Slaveholdings, such as these, made of slavery an institution far different from the slavery of up-country districts, where the hands worked under the close supervision of the owner. On the large plantations the slaves worked under drivers, overseers, and occasionally stewards, seldom seeing the master unless chosen for personal service. They lived an isolated life with little opportunity of learning the ways of the outside world.

During the ante-bellum régime the average size of landholding on the Island was 573 acres. Of forty landholders thirty held between one hundred and one thousand acres while only four held less than a hundred and six held more than a thousand acres. It was seldom, however, that a planter worked his land in tracts larger than a few hundred acres. Captain John Fripp's 2,210 acres were divided into seven plantations. Sometimes a planter's tracts were separated by three or four miles.

Here, as in the rest of the sea island cotton area, was the quintessence of large scale plantation economy. Large landholdings and large slaveholdings were concentrated in the hands of a few wealthy persons who built fine houses in Beaufort for their summer residences and for the winter had plantation houses on the Island. They furnished their homes with Turkish carpets, marble mantels, rosewood and mahogany furniture, oil paintings, and fine books; they educated their sons in the best colleges in this country and abroad, and the sons returned, doctors, ministers, authors, to build their share of the inheritance into a new plantation patriarchy.

The characteristic plantation system of the Sea Islands evolved out of the production of long staple cotton. The average sea island planter cultivated a little less than six acres to the hand. In addition to cotton, he raised corn and sweet potatoes as provision crops in the proportion of about seven-twelfths cotton, three-twelfths corn, and two-twelfths sweet potatoes. The average yield of cotton was about 135 pounds to the acre; of corn, fifteen to twenty-five bushels of the southern white-flint variety; and of potatoes, about 150 bushels to the acre. Other tasks there were for slave hands to do, the care of cattle and poultry, building and repair work, domestic service, but these were all subordinate to the production of cotton.

During the slack season in summer or in the late fall and winter months slaves went out in boats upon the tidal creeks and "bogged" the marshes for grass and mud to add humus and fertilizer to the soil in preparation for the crop. A mixture of marsh grass, mud, and barnyard manure was applied to the fields at the rate of about forty cart loads to the acre, the amount of compost and the proportion of ingredients being suited to the character of the land. Some planters also added broken shells because of their lime content. Just before the Civil War a few experimented with commercial fertilizer, but never to any great extent.

Gathering marsh was an arduous task. After it had been brought to shore, instead of being "composted," it was often hauled in carts or toted in woven baskets directly to the field where it was spread by hand and later listed in with the previous year's growth. This method of fertilization continues to this day, each small landholder going out with his children to the marsh instead of in a party of stout men as in slavery days.

The planting season began in February with the listing of the soil in preparation for drilling the cotton seed in late March or early April in ridges four or five feet apart. After the plants were up they were hoed at frequent intervals until July when all work on the crop ceased until September. From then until December the crop was harvested, the fields being frequently gone over to save the fiber which was quickly damaged by bad weather.

While some hands were busy in the fields, others were

at work in the gin houses at the tedious process of preparing the staple for market. The cotton on being gathered was dried on a scaffold inside the gin house, sent to the whipper, which extracted the sand and imperfect fibers, and then assorted according to color and fineness before being taken to the gin. Whitney's tooth gin, which was used for upland cotton, broke the delicate fibers of sea island cotton. This staple was separated from the seed by being passed between hardwood rollers propelled by foot power. Again unlike upland cotton, which was ready for market when ginned, sea island had to be processed still further. The ginned cotton was carefully moted and then finally packed into round bags of about three hundred pounds, fifteen hundred pounds of seed cotton being required for a bale of this size.

It usually cost a planter about twenty-seven dollars a bale to process his cotton in this way. Such an operation was obviously most economical when associated with large scale production. When the plantations were abolished on St. Helena Island and the Negroes began small scale production on their little ten- and twenty-acre lots, they could not afford to buy equipment to process their cotton. This function was assumed by one of the large mercantile establishments of the Island which operated a gin and bought the seed cotton from the Negroes.

But careful processing was not always a guarantee of fine cotton. The plant was subject to blight, rust, blue, and it was frequently attacked by cut worm, plant louse and leaf worm, or caterpillar. The weather, too, often conspired against the crop. A late frost in the spring might require a re-planting; an early frost in autumn might

COTTON AND "CONTRABANDS" 27

shorten the crop by many bales; mid-season rains or hailstorms might cause the plant to shed its fruit; or autumnal hurricanes might completely destroy the crop. The sea island cotton planter, like the grower of upland cotton, played a game of chance with nature, but the sea island planter played at greater hazards because his plant was more delicate.

The uncertainty of the crop, the constant and often great fluctuations in the price, together with the large investment of capital in land and slaves required to cultivate the crop at a profit, caused a rising tide of discontent as early as the thirties which became more pronounced as the antebellum period wore on. A planter might have from $50,000 to $100,000 invested in his plantation, but even if well managed he might not hope to receive a high percentage on the investment. The account book of one of these well-managed plantations shows that over a period of forty years the owner realized only 4.4 per cent on his capital without any allowance of a salary for himself as supervisor.

With so small a profit as this, it is no wonder that planters complained of the unsuccessfulness of sea island cotton planting and tried to find a way out of the difficulty. The agricultural journals of the time show the planters' efforts to improve upon their methods of cultivation. They wrote articles, circulated questionnaires, and organized agricultural societies. They discussed rotation of crops, soil analysis, better methods of fertilization and tillage, but only the most energetic availed themselves of this new information. It seldom occurred to a planter to reduce his acreage in cotton and make his plantation first of all self-supporting so that in the lean years he would not have to go heavily in debt to his factor. Instead, he continued to buy many of his provisions, his bacon, corn, and rice, from his factor, and continued to put as many acres as possible in cotton.

A few acute planters were quick to realize that many of the failures in cultivating sea island cotton were inherent in the system itself. As early as 1834 Whitemarsh B. Seabrook, writing for the *Southern Agriculturist*, lay the chief blame to the planter's mismanagement: to his absence from the plantation in the summer months, to his want of strict personal supervision when he was at home, to his over-planting, and to his ignorance.

St. Helena planters quite generally employed overseers to supervise the detailed operations of their plantations, while they were content to spend "the sickly season" at Beaufort or at the North, remaining on their plantations sometimes less than half the year. Toward the close of the slavery régime, a few had begun to realize the inefficiency of this plan and they built a summer resort at St. Helenaville, supposedly one of the Island's healthiest spots.

Good overseers were hard to get and harder to keep because the really successful ones were likely to start planting for themselves. The overseer's position was a difficult one, for his employer expected him not only to manage the plantation economically and raise a good crop, but also to keep the Negroes satisfied and happy. For the most part they were ill fitted for their positions, ignorant, crude, and poorly paid.

Immediately under the overseer were the drivers, trusted slaves who were given a certain amount of authority over the others. It was the driver's business to superintend generally the work of the field hands. He issued rations; he saw that each laborer's work was properly performed; and he inflicted punishment whenever he saw fit, always, however, subject to the overseer's or master's orders. In their absence, he usually succeeded to much of their authority. Many of the abuses of slave management on a large scale arose through the officiousness of these drivers, for it was easy for them, in their positions of power, to work off private pique or to display favoritism. A missionary on St. Helena Island in the early days of the Civil War described a driver on one of the plantations as possessing a " 'cuteness and big eye to his own advantage." One of the "grand points" in plantation management, therefore, was to select capable drivers and place sufficient checks upon their authority.

Next to the driver, in privilege and esteem, were the mechanics and house servants, the "swonga" Negroes who looked askance at the field hands. From among his people, the planter not only chose a few to render personal service to his own family but he also delegated a cook, house boy, and perhaps a coachman to wait upon his overseer. The mechanics did the carpenter work for the plantation and in slack seasons were hired out to others.

Less than half of a planter's total number of slaves could be depended upon for a full day's work, for his possession included the young, the old, and the sick. When Captain Basil Hall toured the United States in 1827 and 1828, he found 122 slaves on a sea island plantation which he visited. Of these, seventy were men and women between the ages of fourteen and fifty; forty-eight were children under the age of fourteen; and four were superannuated. The seventy workers were classified as follows: thirty-nine full hands, sixteen three-quarter hands, eleven half hands, and four quarter hands. Out of 122 slaves, therefore, the planter had fifty-seven and a half "taskable hands," of whom forty-four worked in the fields and the other thirteen and a half were employed as cart drivers, nurses, cooks for the Negroes, carpenters, house servants, and stock minders.

The basis of work on the plantation was the task. In time the term came to signify a quarter of an acre laid out 105 by 105 feet. The number of tasks for a full hand each day depended upon the time of year and the kind of work he was doing. At listing and hauling in preparation for planting, the assignment was usually one task; at planting it was usually three tasks, and at hoeing two tasks. Other phases of plantation work were likewise estimated on the basis of their difficulty.

Most of the plantation work was performed with the simplest of farm implements, the hoe, axe, and spade. The draft animals were more likely to be oxen than mules.

The amount and character of food supplied slaves varied with the plantation, but most sea island planters based the rations on corn and sweet potatoes with an occasional allowance of meat and molasses. The variations were provided by peas, rice, salt fish, and soup. On the tide rivers, planters encouraged their slaves to supplement their rations with fish, oysters, and crabs, and they permitted each family to have poultry, a pig, and a garden with the right to sell the products as "nigger truck" to the master or the small stores, and to use the proceeds to buy other articles of food if they chose. Thomas A. Coffin, a St. Helena planter, regularly issued to each of his two hundred slaves a peck of corn a week, and from April to June when work was heavy two pecks of corn and two and a half pounds of bacon. Besides, he killed twelve beeves for them in summer and four at Christmas and issued four barrels of molasses in summer. He allowed every hand a quart of salt a month and every man two "hands" of tobacco a month and four "hands" at Christmas.

The yearly supply of clothing which this same planter issued amounted to an impressive bill of goods. In April he gave out 500 yards of men's blue cotton cloth, 600 yards of coarse unbleached shirting, 600 yards of material for women's underclothes, 600 yards of gay calico for frocks, 100 handkerchief pieces, and 100 straw hats; in November, 550 yards of stout woolen for men's clothes, 600 yards of thinner woolen for women, 1,200 yards of unbleached cloth for shirts and underclothes, 100 turban handkerchiefs, 100 warm caps, 200 pairs of shoes, and 67 blankets, with additional hose and flannels for the drivers, mechanics, and house servants.

The type of houses which the master provided his people depended upon his prosperity and his plantation management. Observers sometimes reported that the cabins were "ill conditioned being without chimneys," sometimes that they were "wretched hovels," and again that the "cottages" might "have shamed those of many countries."

A coastal planter estimated in 1844 for the South Carolina Agricultural Society that at the prices then prevailing it cost $17.64 a year to feed and clothe a slave. This estimate was based upon commodity prices much lower than the present. For instance, it included homespun at 10 cents a yard, shoes at 90 cents a pair, and bacon at 4½ cents a pound. Upon adding to this estimate the expense of providing a house, medical care, and incidentals one finds that the cost to the master amounted to a little less than $50. When it is remembered that two or more slaves were fed and clothed for every "taskable hand," it will be seen that the cost per hand ran between $75 and $100 a year, equivalent to wages of about $7 or $8 a month. In 1860 day laborers were receiving in South Carolina 77 cents a day without board and farm hands $10.37 a month with board, only a few dollars more than it cost to support a slave. When it is considered that slaves, unskilled and poorly supervised, cultivated only six acres to the hand, it will be seen that the plantation operated not only at a low wage level, but also at a low level of efficiency, even when compared with the indifferent tenant farming of the cotton belt today.

The health of the slaves was a particular care of the master, the overseer, and often the mistress. Some owners contracted with physicians for the medical care of their plantations at a flat rate per head for the year, and most planters were themselves skilled in simple medicine, keeping at hand such compendiums as Dr. J. Hume Simon's *The Planter's Guide, and Family Book of Medicine*, published in Charleston in 1848. All large plantations had hospitals, or "sick houses." That of Hopeton, on the Georgia coast, as described by Sir Charles Lyell, had three wards, one for men, one for general illnesses of women, and one for maternity cases.

The mistress, with the assistance of a midwife, often attended the slave mother at "birthing" a child. The mistress herself seldom had the ministrations of a physician on such occasions. It was the mistress' duty to instruct the midwives carefully, and the master presented the Negro nurses with fifty cents or a dollar at Christmas for every live birth, as a reward for their skill. He also frequently gave the slave mother a bonus for children surviving until their first birthdays.

Nevertheless, the general level of health for both white people and Negroes in the Sea Islands was low, but the whites escaped the "sickly season" by retiring to the health-resort towns. Malaria, smallpox, "peri-pneumonia," yellow fever, typhoid, cholera, and infant's diseases took heavy toll.

The records of Wehaw plantation, near Georgetown, S. C., show that in a slave population averaging 270, over a period of sixteen years, there was an average of eighty-nine births per thousand and eighty-three deaths per thousand.[3] The marvelous fecundity maintained the natural increase of six per year per thousand in spite of the frightful death rate.

In the economic life of the plantation there may be found the origins of many habits of the people of St. Helena today. The plantation system made them satisfied with a low standard of living, the bare necessities of food, clothing, and shelter. It fixed their habits of laying out

[3] These records do not indicate whether still births were included but the probability is that they were.

the fields, of fertilizing and tilling the soil, of placing their main dependence upon cotton, and of relying upon someone else to process it for market. It began moulding their health habits.

The plantation was not only an economic unit, but a social community as well. Most planters exercised as little supervision as necessary over the social life of their people. The slave's task was not heavy. Smart hands were often through by two o'clock; only the sluggards remained until four or five. When the task was finished, the rest of the day was theirs to spend as they chose. Then, living began in the slave street. This was the time for marriaging, housekeeping, gardening, funeralizing, praising, and pleasuring. There was here a well-marked, if rudimentary, community life among these isolated sea island Negroes who were described by observers as backward, even when compared to the slaves of the inland counties.

St. Helena planters quite generally required their people to choose mates for life. They encouraged pre-nuptial engagements and required marriage ceremonies with varying degrees of solemnity. Many mates were faithful for life, but others did not share the monogamous views of the master. Contemporary preachers and the planters themselves complained frequently of the lightness of the marriage yoke upon slaves. This is not remarkable when one considers that they were but a few generations from African polygamy, that the law did not recognize or protect slave marriages, that the master, ever solicitous for an increasing population, cared for the "bush" children as carefully as for the legitimate.

In the plantation domestic establishment, the woman was supreme. The cabin was hers, and the children hers to name and discipline. The driver usually issued the weekly rations to her, and she pounded the corn into grits and cooked the meals. She tended the "patch" back of the cabin, the pig, and the poultry with the casual assistance of her husband and children. She made the family clothes unless a seamstress performed this function for the whole plantation. If she could economize on the rations in order to have some left at the end of the week to turn back, or if she had surplus truck or poultry to sell, the money was hers to hoard or to purchase extra delicacies. She cared for the children after her task was finished, but when she was in the field the older children and the plantation nurses took them in charge.

In fact, so dependent upon the women were the men of the plantation that freedom from female domination was one of the first and most prized results of emancipation. Miss Laura M. Towne, a missionary to St. Helena Island after the Federal occupation in 1861, wrote, "The notion of being bigger than women generally is just now inflating the conceit of the males to an amazing degree."

It took very little to "pleasure" a slave. He was fond of fishing along the bank for the great variety of fish and shell fish which abounded in the salt water creeks. He would have liked to go out upon the water in a boat to fish, but this the master would not hear to; nor could he hunt except for rabbits with his dogs, for the law forbade more than one slave on a plantation to carry a gun and that only for the purpose of shooting crows or providing game for the master's table.

Singing and dancing were his chief emotional outlets. The preachers and ministers were prejudiced against the "heathenish" violin, so that vocal music became the mode. Yet one planter who had been having trouble with discipline found that his difficulties ended when he provided fiddles and drums to promote dancing. The slaves' dance was a sort of group shuffle performed by the crowd rather than in couples. It was held sometimes in the open and sometimes in one of the cabins where the entire adult group would gather and shuffle all night in the reddish glare of the "lightwood" fire which threw its grotesque shadows across the walls.

Singing and dancing were inextricably interwoven. Miss Frederika Bremer, who came to the United States to observe the homes of the new world, was impressed by this fact. "One must see these people singing if one is rightly to understand their life," she wrote. "They sang so that it was a pleasure to hear, with all their souls and with all their bodies in unison; for their bodies wagged, their heads nodded, their feet stamped, their knees shook, their elbows and their hands beat time to the tune and words which they sang with evident delight."

Planters regularly allowed their people Saturday afternoon and Sunday for rest as well as three days at Christmas and a day after each season of heavy work. These were the most frequent opportunities for visits off the plantation. Most planters, however, issued leave grudgingly except to the most trusted slaves, for they did not wish to encourage inter-plantation visiting.

Since the time of worship was one of the most frequently recurring opportunities to gather, it is but natural that the slaves should take advantage of it to add a recreational feature, the "shout," which differed little from the dance except that it was held in the praise house at the close of the devotion. The praise house was the plantation church, sometimes the cabin of the religious leader, at other times a building which the master had erected especially for that purpose. The leaders of these praise houses, sometimes licensed preachers, were persons of considerable authority and often settled disputes as well as solemnized weddings and funerals. They organized the church members into a class and presided over it, as the class leader in the white churches; but the Reverend C. C. Jones and other ante-bellum ministers were of the opinion that the Negro leaders perverted their religious practices with African superstitions.

Planters usually encouraged the various denominations to send missionaries among their people. As early as the thirties, ministers had prepared and published special sermons, "dialogues," and catechisms for colored people. On St. Helena most of the slaves adhered to the Baptist denomination because their masters were of that faith. Edward L. Pierce, who visited St. Helena soon after the Federal occupation in 1861, remarked that he found an abundance of Baptist literature lying about in the homes of the planters.

Through the church a limited number of Negroes learned to read and write in Sunday schools, although this movement was largely abandoned after 1835 when the planters began to fear the results of the abolition movement.

The rudimentary social organization among the slave people of the plantation may be traced to this day in many of the customs of St. Helena: the divided responsibility for farm duties between the man and the woman, the high illegitimacy rate, the praise house, the shout, and the authority of the church in governing conduct.

The slave community was not disrupted when the masters fled and the Federal agents came. It continued more or less undisturbed with the authority and supervision shifted to new white controllers.

The fall of Port Royal placed behind the Union lines some ten thousand Negroes whose status was doubtful. "Contrabands of War," General Butler had called the slaves within his lines when he had captured Hampton Roads, and contrabands they were at Port Royal. How could they be fed and clothed in the absence of their masters? Who would direct their work? How would their attitude toward the new authority be guided? These and a dozen other puzzling questions confronted the army of occupation.

The War Department shifted the burden to the Treasury Department, but it could not refrain from meddling. It scoured the plantations for boats and mules for transportation service and corn and cattle for the commissary. Then when the Treasury agents had got the crops well under way in 1862, an order came for all men between eighteen and forty-five to report for military service, and six hundred prime hands were taken from their plantation homes on St. Helena alone.

The Treasury hastily appointed agents to collect the bountiful cotton crop which the planters had left in the fields and in the meantime selected Edward L. Pierce, a

COTTON AND "CONTRABANDS" 39

lawyer of Boston, to visit the conquered territory and devise some scheme for taking care of the Negroes. Pierce found the Negroes dissatisfied with the treatment they were receiving at the hands of the soldiers and the cotton agents, and he at once disapproved of the plan which had already been proposed to lease the plantations with the people on them to the highest bidders.

Instead, he conceived of a social experiment whereby the Treasury Department would cultivate the plantations under a system of superintendents, carefully chosen, their chief object being "to promote the moral and intellectual culture of the wards" and "to prepare them for useful and worthy citizenship." The slaves should be kept at their accustomed tasks but their incentive should be wages instead of the lash. With the superintendents there should go ministers and teachers to instruct the contrabands in the ways of civilization. Thus the Negro's capacity for citizenship would be tested and some conclusion reached as to the policy to be pursued toward him at the close of the war.

On March 9 a band of superintendents and teachers, led by Pierce, reached Beaufort and two weeks later they were at their posts. The North had caught enthusiastically at the idea and organized benevolent societies to help with the work. These societies not only furnished large quantities of food and clothing for the Negroes but they assumed payment of the superintendents' salaries for a few months and kept teachers in the field until long after the war.

The superintendent's task was a difficult one. He generally had five or six plantations in charge, and sometimes, with the assistance of a teacher, had as many as five hundred Negroes under his supervision. He found the Negroes suspicious of the "foreigners," discontented with the "confusion," and unwilling to cultivate cotton. He had to explain to them their own new condition and the purposes of the Government toward them, urge them to work the Government land as well as their own private patches, equip the plantations with implements from the Government storehouses, procure and distribute food whenever the army issued rations or the benevolent societies sent supplies, draw pay rolls for labor on cotton, pay the amounts and settle the disputes which inevitably arose, and in general supervise the social and religious life of the Negroes.

Although the superintendents were for the most part capable men, they had an almost impossible task to perform. They knew nothing of the system of agriculture which they were supposed to supervise; they could not get the cooperation of headquarters; and they could not "satisfy" their laborers. The Negroes "are crying loudly & with some reason, that we don't treat them so well as their old masters," wrote a superintendent to Pierce. "They have no salt [,] no molasses, sugar or fresh meat. They see the soldiers kill their cattle & sit in idleness (as it seems to them) while their masters gave them a beef once a month & an allowance of the other luxuries." A great reduction in the cotton crop showed the effects of this disorganization. Whereas the Government had received two hundred thousand dollars from the planters' crops of 1861, it realized scarcely more than forty thousand dollars from the crops of 1862.

In June, 1862, the "experiment" was transferred from the Treasury to the War Department, and Brigadier-General Rufus Saxton placed in command. Pierce was offered

COTTON AND "CONTRABANDS" 41

a place on his staff with the rank of colonel, but foreseeing, no doubt, that the plan of the experiment was soon to be altered, he declined the appointment. General Saxton inherited the confusion which Pierce had found harmful to the successful cultivation of the plantations and which in his brief command he was unable to overcome.

The next two years saw many changes in the method of dealing with the contrabands. For the crop of 1863, Saxton, at the suggestion of some of the superintendents, ordered that the plantations be divided into plots and rented without charge to the Negro families unless they refused to cultivate cotton, in which case they should be required to pay a rent of about two dollars a month. In addition, the Government furnished implements and seeds and paid twenty-five cents a day for labor. In March, 1863, the conquered territory was sold at auction for the Federal direct tax levied by the act of August 5, 1861. Some of the plantations were bid in by the Government and others sold to private individuals. The Government plantations were leased to approved persons, usually the superintendents and teachers who had previously supervised them, but all superintendents whether of privately owned or of Government owned plantations were required to file a signed statement with one of Saxton's deputies concerning the terms of their agreement with the laborers.

The authority by which the Government sold 110,000 acres of land in Beaufort District and the entire town of Beaufort for the Federal direct tax was the act of June 7, 1862, calling for the appointment of direct tax commissioners to collect the tax in the eleven insurrectionary states. Commissioners sold land for the non-payment of taxes in Virginia, Florida, Arkansas, Tennessee, and South Carolina, but only in South Carolina was there put into operation a plan whereby Negroes became landowners.

Most of the land at Port Royal was sold for taxes in March, 1863. The Government bid in about two-thirds of the amount and loyal citizens of the North the remainder. In September, 1863, the President issued instructions reserving thirty-six tracts of 160 acres each for school farms, the profits of which were to go to the education of the Negro, and certain other tracts for "heads of families of the African race." The land reserved for the Negroes was to be divided into ten-acre lots and sold at not less than $1.25 an acre, one lot to each head of a family "for the charitable purpose of providing homes." In December the sales to heads of families had begun and were continued at irregular intervals until 1870 when the board of commissioners was dissolved. By June, 1865, there had been 347 purchasers on St. Helena Island. Of this number 243 bought ten acres, 166 paying $1.50 an acre and 72 paying $1.25, the other five paying from $2 to $6.50 an acre. The highest price paid for any tract was $350 for twenty acres. The commissioners sold buildings on these tracts at one-third their appraised value.

In 1865 General Sherman, on reaching the sea, issued his famous Special Field Orders No. 15 setting aside "the islands from Charleston, south, the abandoned rice fields along the rivers for thirty miles back from the sea, and the country bordering the St. John's river, Florida," for the freedmen. Under this order many Negroes outside the Port Royal region claimed the right to their masters' lands

COTTON AND "CONTRABANDS" 43

until they were persuaded by officers of the Freedmen's Bureau or by their masters themselves to be satisfied with a contract for labor rather than the title to the soil. To meet this situation Congress, by an amendment to the Freedmen's Bureau Act of 1866, ordered a sale of most of the public land at Port Royal at $1.50 an acre "to such persons and to such only as have acquired and are now occupying lands under and agreeably to the provisions of General Sherman's special field order." This same act called for the sale of the school farms at $10 an acre, setting aside the money arising therefrom for the support of schools in St. Helena's and St. Luke's parishes. By 1867 there were almost two thousand Negro landowners in the region.

The chief white purchaser at the first land sale in 1863 had been Edward S. Philbrick, of Brookline, Mass., who had come out with Pierce as a superintendent. When the Government had abandoned the experiment of training the Negro for citizenship, he decided to carry it on with private funds, and interested a group of New England men to join him in the enterprise. He bought eleven plantations on St. Helena Island at about a dollar an acre and employed superintendents and teachers to work under him, finally selling the land after 1865 to whites and Negroes. At no time after the sale of the land for taxes has St. Helena Island been occupied solely by Negroes. A few plantations have always been in the hands of white owners.

After the war a few masters returned to St. Helena and Beaufort, but by far the greater number went elsewhere trying to rebuild a fortune which had been taken away from them suddenly and dramatically. Most of them had neither the money nor the privilege of reclaiming their lands, for the redemption act of 1872 permitted only such lands as were in Government possession to be reclaimed. They left the region which had been their homes for more than a century to the possession of their former slaves, who, for the most part, carried on the traditions and customs which the plantation system had taught them.

The freedmen of Port Royal found themselves in 1865 prosperous and "fair spoiled." Military officers were especially appointed to see that they were not imposed upon by whites; work was plentiful, and prices high. The presence of the soldiers offered a ready market for whatever they had to sell; the presence of the camps offered jobs at "cash money"; the army offered a bounty of three hundred dollars for all volunteers. Whenever it was possible to peddle chickens, fish, and garden truck to the soldiers, the freedmen never raised cotton. They spent their easily-got money for their own little plot of land and equipped it with a few simple implements, a cart, and a few "critters," pigs, an ox, and perhaps a government-condemned horse. Their cabins, which they had either moved from the street or newly built of pine logs, they furnished with beds, chairs, and tables. They must have a few dishes and, perhaps, knives and forks. They indulged themselves, too, with both a work suit and a Sunday suit of clothes.

Soon the freedmen felt the pinch of hard times. A succession of crop failures took what little cash they had hoarded from the flush days and left them facing starvation. White planters and Negro farmers suffered alike. Although some of the Negroes cultivated their fields carefully after the methods learned during slavery, the majority were slip-shod. "The Negroes' crops did not turn out very well, as a general rule," wrote a white planter from St. Helena, "want of manure and careless working being the principal causes." Gathering marsh grass and mud for their fields was an arduous task which most of them wished to avoid. Much of the fine seed, too, had been lost during the Federal occupation. This fact added to careless working caused the fiber to deteriorate and prices to fall lower than they ordinarily would have in the post-war deflation. The Negro farmer was further handicapped by the fact that he had to sell his cotton in the seed because he did not have the equipment with which to process it.

But cotton remained the Islander's chief money crop until its destruction by the boll weevil in 1918. In the autumn after the cotton had been gathered he had a little money with which to pay taxes and buy a few clothes, but during the rest of the year he lived without money. Yet there were some who prospered. At the close of the reconstruction period, small two-story houses with porches, window panes, and a neat coat of paint had begun to appear on the Island.

Twice since their freedom, the St. Helena people have suffered severe reverses by hurricanes accompanied by tidal waves. The storm of 1893 carried away crops, homes, and animals, and many a family suffered the loss of some member. The tidal wave of 1911 was less disastrous but it left many homeless and penniless.

No work which Pierce undertook in his social experiment of 1862 appealed to the Negroes as much as did the schools. The slates and books which the benevolent societies sent seemed to them a proof of the Yankees' sincerity. By 1864 there were thirty schools in the conquered territory, taught by some forty teachers with an average attendance of two thousand pupils. Even adults went to school after their day's work was done. These first schools were opened by the Northern benevolent societies, but in 1864 the Government conducted schools in the districts of the school farms and in 1866 created a Federal fund, with the money arising from the sale of the school farms, for "the support of schools, without distinction of color or race, on the islands in the parishes of Saint Helena and Saint Luke." State schools were opened on St. Helena in 1874.

Among the first group of teachers to reach St. Helena in 1862 was Miss Laura M. Towne of Philadelphia. Later in the year she was joined by her friend Miss Ellen Murray and together they taught a school at the Oaks plantation out of which there finally evolved the present Penn Normal, Industrial, and Agricultural School which has had so important an effect upon the life of the entire Island.

The Civil War saw little change in the social life of the Negro. Pierce had ordered that all marriages be performed according to law, but the freedman had little more respect for this form of marriage than he had for the marriages of plantation days. As in slavery, the praise leaders had attempted to regulate the affairs of the members, so in freedom the officers of the praise house and the church sought to smooth out all the private and public disputes arising on the Island. The passage of years brought

COFFIN PLANTATION

SCREENED WITH FIGS AND POMEGRANATES

changes, but the people in their isolation were slow to give up their traditions. Their folk-ways were the outgrowth of slavery; their songs, the ones they had sung in bondage; their speech, the English their ancestors had learned when they were "tamed."

CHAPTER III

ST. HELENA SONGS AND STORIES [1]

Lord, I can't help from singing sometimes,
Lord, I can't help from singing sometimes,
When my heart is full of fears
And my eyes are dim with tears,
Lord, I can't help from singing sometimes.

Buh Rahbit an' Buh Wolf all-two go fuh hunt deah. Buh Wolf got plenty gunjuh an' 'e buy 'im one dog, but Buh Rahbit ent got mo' 'n one gunjuh, so 'e buy 'im one dog haid. Dey ent gone too long 'fo' Buh Wolf dog run a deah. Buh Rahbit say, "Come on, Buh Wolf, my dog haid done ketch 'um," an' 'e run ahaid o' Buh Wolf an' knock Buh Wolf dog off de deah an' fasten de dog haid on de deah, an' w'en Buh Wolf git deh Buh Rahbit tell 'um, say, "Look, Buh Wolf, my dog haid kill deah." Buh Wolf say, "Dog haid cyan' kill deah. Tek a dog fuh kill deah." Buh Rahbit say, "Oh, yeh, dog haid kill deah. Yunnah shum deh on de deah, enty? 'E *my* deah, an' I gwine git a cyaat fuh fetch 'um home." W'ile Buh Rahbit been attah de cyaat, Buh Wolf been a-study. Finally at las' 'e yeddy Buh Rahbit duh come wid de cyaat, an' 'e tek a piece o' grape-wine an' biggin fuh beat on a tree an' cry, "Please, Maussa, please don' beat we! My dog ent ketch yunnah deah. Buh Rahbit dog haid ketch dat deah. Oh, please, Maussa!" Buh Rahbit hice 'e yehs an' listen. Buh Wolf

---

[1] This chapter is a summary of the data on folk culture. For more detailed treatment, one may refer to the volume on folk backgrounds by Guy B. Johnson; or to such works as *Gullah*, by Reed Smith, University of South Carolina; *St. Helena Island Spirituals*, by N. G. J. Ballanta; and *Folklore of the Sea Islands, S. C.*, by Elsie Clews Parsons.

keep on fuh hollah. Buh Rahbit jump off de cyaat and call out, say, "Oh, Buh Wolf, you lie. Whoebbah yeard of a dog haid ketch deah. Dog haid cyan' ketch deah, tek a dog fuh ketch deah." An' 'e run off an' lef' 'um fo' Buh Wolf.

The charm of the folk stories of the sea island people is inseparably bound up with the staccato tones of their speech and the quaintness of their idiom. The foregoing specimen of dialect represents the speech of those who have come under the modifying influence of education. The first impression of the newcomer upon hearing the old-timers talk is apt to be that he is listening to a foreign language. There are older Negroes in the Sea Islands who speak in such a way that a stranger would have to stay around them several weeks before he could understand them and converse with them to his satisfaction.

But this strange dialect turns out to be little more than the peasant English of two centuries ago, modified to suit the needs of the slaves. From Midland and Southern England came planters, artisans, shopkeepers, indentured servants, all of whom had more or less contact with the slaves, and the speech of these poorer white folk was so rustic that their more cultured countrymen had difficulty in understanding them. From this peasant speech and from the "baby talk" used by masters in addressing them, the Negroes developed that dialect, sometimes known as Gullah, which remains the characteristic feature of the culture of the Negroes of coastal South Carolina and Georgia.

When the Sea Islander pronounces words like *man, back, plant, rabbit* with a broad *a*, and words like *heart, cart, spark* with a very prolonged flat *a*, he is merely following patterns which his forefathers learned from the early white settlers. Queer combinations result from these pronunciations: a *dark man* is a *daak mon* and *marsh land* is *maash lon'*. Likewise *pless* for *place, deesh* for *dish, coe* for *cow, bile* for *boil, onlock* for *unlock,* and many others are pronunciations which were once widely used by the white people. Indeed, most of them can still be heard among the less sophisticated whites of the South.

Shifting of consonants leads to some unusual pronunciations. *B* and *v are* interchanged, for *neighbor* is often *neighvuh,* while *Venus* is sometimes *Benus.* As with some of Dickens' characters, *w* and *v are* frequently interchanged. *Voice* becomes *woice, visitor* is *wisituh. Grapevine* becomes *grape-wine,* and if the speaker means *grape-wine* he says *grape-vine.* These, together with other consonantal peculiarities, such as *islant* for *island, w'ite* for *white, squestion* for *question, yeye* for *eye, gyaaden* for *garden,* are all derived from English dialect. Some of these, like the *y* sound inserted in such words as *car* and *garden,* are also characteristic of the speech of the lowcountry white aristocracy.

Even the substitution of *t* and *d* for the *th* sounds, as typified by *dis* for *this* and *t'ick* for *thick,* can as easily be attributed to the rustic speech of Kent and Sussex as to the fact that the *th* sounds are lacking in most of the African tongues. Similarly an intrusive *n*, as in *nyoung* for *young, nused* for *used,* is as well explained by the English dialect usage as by the fact that in many African words an *n* sound is prefixed to an initial consonant, as in *Ngola, Ndulamo,* etc.

The elimination of prefixes, the combining of several

ST. HELENA SONGS AND STORIES

words into one, and the mutilation or corruption of words are carried to the extreme in the sea island dialect, yet a study of English dialect shows that the English yeomanry were given to the same habits. In fact, most of the words thus affected in the Negro dialect can be traced specifically to English patterns. When the Negro says *sump'n'-nurrah* for *something or other,* *tummuch* for *too much,* *argufy* for *argue,* *sparrowgrass* for *asparagus,* he is merely repeating words which his forefathers took over from their English associates in the early days of slavery.

The grammar of the dialect is a simplified English grammar taken over from the speech of the poorer whites. Distinctions of person, number, gender, case, and tense are reduced to the minimum. *He* or *'e* does service for *he, she, it.* A woman is usually *he:* "Mary, 'e ent feel so good." Yet a man is likely to call his ox or his bull *she.* One is reminded of the remark cited by Halliwell, an authority on the dialects of England, that in Hampshire "everything is called *he* except a tom-cat which is called *she.*"

"He brudduh dog" means "his brother's dog," "we house" means "our house," for the sign of the possessive is nearly always omitted. Possessor and possessed are often separated by many words. A man was asked, "Is that your goat over there?" and he replied, "No, suh, dat de mon whut lib obuh deh een dat nex' house weh yunnah been to de fun'ral las' week goat."

"De roostuh crow" may mean one rooster or a dozen roosters, for plurals mean nothing. An ox is apt to be "one oxin" but several oxen are designated by "t'ree ox," "five ox," etc.

Expressions like "him say to we," "dem catch up wid he," etc., are typical of the confusion of pronouns. *Um* is a sort of catch-all for *her, it, him, them.* Thus " 'e got um" may mean that he, she, or it gets, or got, it, him, her, or them. "I shum" (from "I see um") serves for I see, saw, will see it, him, her, them.

One verbal ending does duty for all tenses, although the speaker will sometimes emphasize the future by prefixing *gwine*, as in "I gwine run," or the past by *been*, as in "him been-uh laugh at me." Adjectives and nouns do verb service just as in English dialect. A man may *happy* himself, or *pleasure* himself or go *foolishing* around. On making a loan, one man asked for a mortgage "on sump'n whut cyan't *dead*."

All-two and *enty* are much-used expressions. *All-two* is an obsolete form of *both*. *Enty* is used like French *n'est-ce-pas* and German *nicht wahr*. Thus: "gwine rain, enty?" "Dem was good apple, enty?" *Ent* (or *yent*) is also used for *ain't*. The source of *enty* was the *ent, yent, yunt, yunti*, etc., which the English dialect speakers used for *isn't, wasn't, hasn't*, etc.

Perhaps the flavor of the dialect will stand out better if some characteristic phrases be listed.

'E yent specify: he failed to make good, said of persons or things that fall short.
Tek care mo' bettuh nuh beg pardon: to take care is better than to have to say "Beg pardon."
Mos' kill bud don' mek soup: almost killing a bird doesn't make soup.
Fin'lly at las': finally.

Crack 'e teet' (also *breat'*): crack his teeth (or breath), that is, to say something.
'E haak but 'e yent yeddy: he hearkens but doesn't hear, that is, he hears but doesn't heed.
Onrabble 'e mout': unravel his or her mouth, become very talkative.
Keepin' stepney fum de do': keeping the wolf from the door.
Dat gal too shut-mout': she is too secretive, unsociable.
Day clean: full daylight.
Fus' daak: first dark, twilight.
Ractify een 'e min': confused in his mind. Also said of anything which breaks down, as "de boat ractify."

The use of many archaic English words no doubt contributes to the belief held in some quarters that the sea island Negroes use many African words. There are perhaps a hundred of these archaisms, some of which survive only in this dialect, while others are common among the white people in various sections, but especially in the Appalachians and Ozarks. Many of these words are merely outgrown standard English words, having been used by men like Chaucer, Jonson, and Shakespeare. Following are a few selected archaic English usages found in the sea island dialect:

All-two: both.
Ax: ask. Not a Negro corruption. Chaucer used *ax,* and many English and American illiterate people still use that form.
Brawtus: something extra, thrown in for good measure.
Chance: a quantity, a considerable amount. "I raised a right good chance o' 'tatuh."
Coz, cous'n: cousin, a form of address as in Shakespeare's day.
Find: to supply with provisions, victuals, etc.
Gaul: swamp.

Gunjuh: ginger or molasses cookies.
Hippo: ipecac.
Killick: an anchor of stone.
Make your manners: used by the Negroes as it was in England: "a command to a child to touch his hat or curtsey in the presence of superiors."
Meet: to find, to observe, to experience. "Did oona meet a good time?" The fisherman is asked, "Did oona meet plenty feesh?"
Peruse: to saunter, walk leisurely.
Piggin: small wooden pail with one stave extended for a handle.
Quizzet: to question closely.
Soon: early, quick, alert.
Start-naked: stark-naked, probably a direct descendant of Anglo-Saxon *steort-naket,* i.e., *tail-naked.*
Titty: sister.
Too: very.
Use: to frequent or roam over a certain area, as of game, cattle, etc. Used by Spenser, Milton, Shakespeare, and others. Still used by many Southern white people.
Yowe: ewe.

There are surprisingly few African words in this Negro dialect. Such words as *goober, yam, okra,* which are all probably of African derivation, are used, not only by the sea island Negroes, but also widely by white people. About the only African words which are more or less confined to the low country are *buckra* (white man), and possibly *oona* (you), *nyam* (to eat), *ki* (an exclamation), and *plat-eye* (a ghost). The last named is common around Georgetown, but not on St. Helena. There may be a few others, but they are used very locally. The word *Gullah,* by which the whites designate the low-country Negroes and

ST. HELENA SONGS AND STORIES

their speech, is, of course, very likely a corruption of African *Ngola* (*Angola*), *Gola*, or *Gulla*.

Although the phonology and grammar and vocabulary of this dialect can in large measure be traced back to Midland and Southern rural English dialect, the Negro has done something to it which makes it his own. He has given it that indefinable stamp which the members of one linguistic group put upon a strange language. He does not drawl, as most Southerners and up-country Negroes do. His words gush forth in such rapid succession that the newcomer is startled, and he indulges in sudden and extensive changes in vocal pitch which might easily be the counterpart of those musical inflections which are so important in the languages of West Africa.

The teaching of standard English is gradually ironing out the cruder varieties of the dialect. The process is slow, for many teachers in the little island schools teach in the vernacular. Their pupils spell: *m-a-n*, and pronounce *mon*; *h-e-a-r-t*, *haa't*; *w-i-n-d*, *vind*; *v-i-n-e*, *wine*; and will probably go on doing so for years to come. It would really be tragic if the dialect were entirely wiped out by the incursion of standard English, for it is an integral part of the culture of the Islanders. Penn School recognizes this fact and encourages the preservation of the best features of the dialect.

The sea island people are noted for their singing of the old Negro spirituals. In church, in praise house, at school, at home, and at work their voices are often heard intoning the strains of the spirituals. The old and stately hymns of Watts and Wesley are also sung, likewise new choir songs, but the spiritual stands out as the characteristic mode of religious expression of these people.

Secular songs are not nearly as frequent as religious songs on St. Helena Island. In fact, there is a marked paucity of what is usually thought of as the Negro secular song. A few obsolete minstrel and vaudeville songs, a few insignificant songs brought in by returned World War soldiers, some phonograph songs of recent importation, and a dozen or more children's game songs of white descent— these are about the only secular songs sung on the island. It is considered just a little sinful to own a banjo or a guitar, although many families are proud to possess small phonographs.

In the manner of singing the old church hymns the Islanders have perpetuated a technique which goes back to ante-bellum days. The song leader announces the song, gives the meter—purely a matter of form, meaning nothing to the congregation—and lines out a part of the first stanza. This is sung, after which more lines are given out and sung, and so on and on through stanza after stanza of Watts or Wesley. To a "foreigner" the singing may seem painfully slow, for, where it takes the ordinary white church choir about fifteen seconds to sing the first two lines of *Jesus, Lover of My Soul*, it takes these people fifty. High-pitched voices performing upon the prolonged tones of these hymns are singularly lacking in that emotional quality which is associated with the unrestrained singing of spirituals. A few tunes suffice for all hymns, and the monotony of these is scarcely relieved by the attempts at harmony which are made. It is significant of the force of custom that today, when most of the people know the

ST. HELENA SONGS AND STORIES 57

hymns by heart and could sing through them in regular tempo, they go on in the way which their fathers and grandfathers learned during slavery.

Most of the island churches have choirs, composed of singers who have gained some knowledge of sight-singing or are otherwise quick at learning tunes. These choirs use song books of the modern type, and from time to time they introduce new songs to the congregation. The choir songs are of the same type as the songs of the white rural and small-town churches in the South. Indeed, several songs recently introduced to St. Helena are songs which long ago reached their height among white people—for example, *The Fight Is On* and *I Am Bound for the Promised Land*.

It is in singing the spirituals that the Islanders enjoy themselves most. They sing these old songs with a physical and spiritual abandon which makes the performance a self-expressive and satisfying experience.

St. Helena, being an isolated culture area, is an excellent laboratory for the study of the spirituals. Here is found little of that racial inferiority complex which for a time threatened to destroy the spirituals in the up-country, and here there is felt little backwash from the recent exploitation of Negro songs. In such an area certain folk-song traits and processes may be observed more clearly than elsewhere. Some of these may be indicated in the following observations on the St. Helena spirituals.

1. The spirituals of St. Helena are not markedly different from the Negro spirituals as a whole. They are sung in the characteristic sea island dialect, of course, and minor variations occur but fundamentally they are one with Negro spirituals in other parts of the country.

2. The spirituals are sung in unison for the most part. There is very little singing in parts except by the Penn School Quartet and a few other quartets or groups which have practised their songs. Heard from a distance, the singing in praise house or church often gives the impression of multiple part singing, but this effect is more or less of an illusion caused by some of the singers varying the pitch of a given tone or attempting a bit of tenor or alto here, a bit of bass there. Those who look for some weird or new harmonic element contributed to American music by the Negroes of the sea islands will be disappointed, for such harmonies as they do use are in no wise different from conventional white harmonies.

3. There is apparently very little invention or improvisation going on among the island singers. Practically all of the spirituals sung on the Island appear to have originated elsewhere and to have migrated to the sea island region. Because of the continued survival there of many songs rarely heard outside the Sea Islands, it is easy to assume that the songs are indigenous. But recent investigation has shown that these island songs are found among Negroes west of the Appalachians and in an obsolescent state among individuals in the piedmont of Virginia and the Carolinas, which tends to show that the songs originated in the upper South, travelled southward and westward, and are now sung only in a few isolated places.

Perhaps this explains why there is so little mention of local names or incidents in the island spirituals. The St. Helena version of *Roll, Jordan, Roll* tells of "Brother Fuller settin' on de tree of life," referring to the Rev. Richard Fuller, a white Baptist minister who was much esteemed by the slaves. But the tune and stanza pattern of this song probably originated farther north, and the island Negroes merely inserted local names when they learned it. *Don' Let de Win' Blow Heah No Mo'* grew out of the severe storm of 1893, but it appears to have been composed by some individual in Savannah or Charleston.

Although songs were often attributed to local people, only one instance came to the writer's attention in which a person actually claimed authorship. This man frankly said, upon being questioned, that songs known as *his* songs were not his own compositions. He said that they were merely songs which he had "caught" from someone in Savannah or from little "ballets" which he had purchased at some church convention or celebration on the mainland, and had introduced to his church.

4. The secular tendency has not been weeded out of the island spirituals to the same extent that it has among more sophisticated groups. Often when spirituals were being recorded in the outlying schools, stanzas like the following were sung in a perfectly matter-of-fact way:

> See dat man gwine 'cross de fiel'
> Kickin' up dus' like a automobile.
>
> Oh, if I die in Tennessee,
> Don' wan' my friends to grieve attah me.

That the line between religious and secular songs is not always clear was evidenced by the fact that a call for spirituals in the little island schools often brought forth such responses as *The Green Grass Grew All Around* and

Johnny's So Long at the Fair. This sort of thing is, of course, not peculiar to St. Helena, but it is more apparent on the Sea Islands than elsewhere because of the relatively retarded cultural status there.

5. Several variations of the same song occur side by side. For example, *Mary Had a Baby* is sung in three ways, *You Better Run* in three ways, *Wrastlin' Jacob* in two, *Jacob's Ladder* in two, and so on. Of course, this trait is not peculiar to the Sea Islands. In fact the variants of this sort probably originated elsewhere, but they are more apparent on St. Helena because of their convergence and survival there. One rare instance of the origin of a local variant was observed on St. Helena during the past year. In one of the churches a spiritual entitled *You Better Live So Jesus Can Use You* was among the favorites. It was sung rather fast, with pronounced swing and syncopation, the tune being as follows:

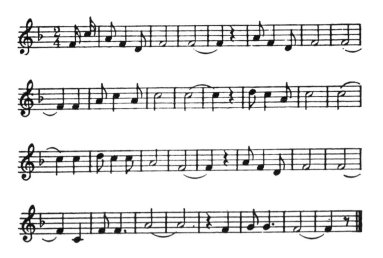

ST. HELENA SONGS AND STORIES

The pastor of another church liked the song, but considered it slightly undignified, so he set to work and revised it to suit his own church. He taught his people to sing it as follows:

6. The same *motif* is found in different tunes, regardless of words, to an unusual extent. This tendency is found in all music, whether it is folk music or art music, but it seems to be especially strong in the spirituals. The writer is convinced that a careful analysis of Negro spirituals will show that less than a hundred separate *motifs* have given rise to over five hundred tunes. The tendency is especially observable on St. Helena because of the convergence and survival of so many types there. A thorough demonstration of this trait of the spirituals would require much space, but a few examples will show what is meant. Take, for example, the instance just cited, where a man

consciously varied a tune. He probably realized that the derived tune was very much like the pattern, but it is doubtful if he saw that his revision is as much like the following tune, *Who's Gwine-a Lay Dis Body Down,* as it is the pattern:

And, to show how complicated this sort of thing may become, the same *motif* crops out again in a spiritual, *Cry Holy Unto de Lawd,* recently introduced from the up-county. Its opening measures are as follows:

To cite one more instance, there is a similarity of *motif* in *Eagle's Wings* and in *My Mother Is Gone an' Lef' Me Behin',* the opening strains of which are, in the order named:

The relationship does not end here, for many readers will at once see the same *motif* in an old white mountain song, *Careless Love,* and some may be able to trace it in still other songs.

A certain St. Helena song leader, at the writer's request, sang a spiritual which he himself had composed. The tune was identical with another St. Helena tune, yet the composer was unaware of the similarity until it had been pointed out to him. Thus musical imagination works and thus new songs arise in old clothes.

7. There is a constant process of change going on among the spirituals. No song has a permanent lease on life, even in isolation. It may be passed on as a "new" song elsewhere, but in its old home it is an "old" song and must compete with newcomers. The collection made by Allen and others and published as *Slave Songs* just after the Civil War contained fifty-five songs from St. Helena. Of these, less than a dozen are commonly heard on the Island today. The present writer returned to St. Helena a year after making his first collection of spirituals there and found several songs in vogue which he never heard once during his first visit. One of these was an old song revived, but the others had come in from "foreign" parts.

Migrants and visitors coming back from Charleston or Savannah or "up North" are constantly introducing new songs.

In this brief summary it is impossible to give an adequate impression of the St. Helena spirituals. For the words and music of a hundred of these songs one may consult the invaluable collection entitled *St. Helena Island Spirituals* (Schirmer, New York, 1925), made by Mr. N. G. J. Ballanta, a native of West Africa.

On the basis of studies of the traits of spirituals, some authors deduced certain theories concerning the relation of the American Negro spiritual to African music. Stated briefly, they are: there is a close relation between the spirituals and African music, in rhythm, in melodic elements, and in form or structure; in other words, the spirituals have certain characteristics which distinguish them from white music and which are ostensibly of African origin. It appears quite likely that these students have neglected to analyse early white religious music for the same traits which, to say the least, casts doubt upon the validity of their conclusions.

First, what are the traits which are supposed to differentiate the spirituals from white music? The leading ones are said to be these:

1. *The use of a gapped scale*, that is, the omission of certain tones from a tune. In *C* scale, for example, the omission of *F*, fourth tone, and *B*, seventh tone, results in what is called the *pentatonic* or five-toned scale. This is supposed to be a particularly distinctive trait of the spirituals. Other frequent gaps are the omission of the fourth tone alone and the omission of the seventh tone alone.

2. *Deviations from our convential scale,* these being the flat seventh tone—in C scale, for instance, using B-flat in a tune where B would conventionally occur—and the neutral third tone, that is, one which, in the scale of C, would fall between E and E-flat.

3. *Rhythmic traits,* as seen in the use of syncopation and the almost exclusive use of two-part time.

4. *The solo-and-chorus form of singing.*

There is a popular belief that the minor mode is a peculiarity of Negro spirituals. Musicians have known better for a long time. About one-tenth of the spirituals are minors, this proportion being actually lower than that found among white religious songs of a century ago.

Now if there is any place in this country where authentic African music traits should have taken root and survived, it should be a place like St. Helena Island. Yet a study of the various collections of spirituals shows (1) that St. Helena spirituals present no striking differences from the other spirituals, (2) that the solo-chorus trait is actually less frequent there than in the upper South, (3) that the proportion of pentatonic tunes is large, but has increased with the infiltration of tunes from farther north.

Perhaps the reason why students of these traits in spirituals have failed to search white music for them is because they thought that there were no comparable white songs. If so they were in error. A little-known segment of white religious history must be mentioned here because it will help to understand not only St. Helena spirituals but the spirituals in general.

As early as Jonathan Edwards' time (1703-1758) there were epidemics of emotional revival meetings in this country, and the common people sang songs of which the more dignified church folk did not approve. This sort of thing appeared from time to time, but in the early 19th century it appeared afresh and swept through the South and West. The descriptions of these camp meetings show the same sort of frenzied preaching, exhorting, and praying, the same sort of shouting, groaning, and bodily exertions, the same sort of simple, repetitive singing which later came to be looked upon as peculiar to Negro revivals. Between 1800 and 1860 dozens of little *"revival songsters"* were published and, in addition, numerous religious folk songs sprang up which were never published, since they were rather undignified and few of the common people could read anyway. In his *American Negro Folk-Songs,* which is the best volume obtainable on the history and present status of Negro songs, Professor Newman I. White has shown conclusively that the white revival songs furnished the pattern for the words of the Negro spirituals. Not only did the revival songs have the same subject matter and the same form as the spirituals, but the latter borrowed many of their most characteristic lines from these songs. Such lines as

> If you get there before I do,
> Look out for me, I'm coming too;
>
> Ride on, Jesus;
>
> We're going to see the bleeding lamb;
>
> You will see the graves a-bursting,

were taken over from white songs. In one small song book published in 1840 the present writer found nearly a hundred lines or couplets which are now sung in Negro spirituals.

But what of the music of the white songs? Studying this is difficult, for so many of the songs were not published, and those that were printed were mostly without the tunes accompanying. A few volumes containing tunes are available, however, and, although they are a little too "highbrow" to be representative of the really folksy type of white religious song, they afford some basis for comparison. Two such volumes (*Christian Lyre*, New York, 18th edition, 1838, and *Millennial Harp*, improved edition, Boston, 1843) have been analyzed statistically. The results may be stated briefly: every deviation from the conventional scale said to be characteristic of Negro spirituals is present in these white songs to about the same extent as in Negro songs, except the use of the pentatonic scale, which occurs in 25 per cent of Negro spirituals in the major mode and in 10 per cent of the white songs in that mode. Those who consider the pentatonic scale as the leading African trait in the spirituals thus receive some confirmation of their belief.

But there is still another angle to the matter of the pentatonic scale. Gapped scales are common in folk music the world over, and the Scotch-Irish brought to this country a wealth of folk song which makes use of gapped scales. It was these same people, in their great migration down the Southern piedmont, who led in the white camp meeting movement, contributing much to its singing and preaching. Throughout the South, and especially in the Appalachians where modern singing has not yet fully penetrated, are found the old English and Scottish ballads and other folk songs which these people brought with them. In these songs occur flat sevenths, neutral thirds, and all the other traits supposed to distinguish Negro music from white music. These traits have been handed down through centuries in England, scarcely touched by the relatively recent development of that conventional music which most of us think of as *the* music.

The pentatonic mode is very frequently used in these English folk songs and in their American derivatives. A comparison of these songs with Negro songs in this respect is given below.

	Per Cent. of Tunes Pentatonic
Krehbiel's analysis of 527 Negro songs (See *Afro-American Folk-Songs*)	21
Fisher's analysis of 574 Negro spirituals (See *Seventy Negro Spirituals*)	35
Campbell & Sharp's *English Folk-Songs from the Southern Appalachians*	25
Richardson & Spaeth's *American Mountain Songs*	21
Reed Smith's *South Carolina Ballads*	28

From this comparison it is obvious that the spirituals have no monopoly on the pentatonic mode. Indeed there is ground for suspicion that the similar proportions of pentatonic tunes in spirituals and in white folk songs are not entirely accidental, for it would be rather strange if a body of folk song with an English heritage and one with an African heritage should by mere chance have so near the same proportion of pentatonic tunes. The same holds good for other traits—absence of seventh tone, absence of fourth tone, flat seventh tone, etc.—for these also occur as frequently in the English-American folk songs as in the spirituals.

But, it will be asked, is there any evidence that Negro tunes were borrowed from white tunes? There is. And this means not merely that instances are known where Negroes have taken over bodily certain tunes which everyone recognizes as white—the traditional English ballads, for example—but that many of their characteristic spirituals are derived from white revival tunes or from other white tunes many of which have become more or less extinct among white people.

The tracing of the relationships between white tunes and Negro tunes is a long story which must be told elsewhere, but one or two examples are in order here. In *Millennial Harp*, a white "songster" already mentioned, is a song called *Mariner's Hymn*. The tune has two very simple and very similar parts. The second part goes as follows:

Oh, I'm come from the land of Egypt! Hallelu-jah! *(repeat)*

This tune was probably derived from an old sailor chantey, for it is similar to one version of *Blow, Boys, Blow*. But what is important here is that the spiritual *I've Been Down Into De Sea* has the same tune:

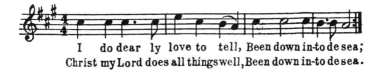
I do dear ly love to tell, Been down in-to de sea;
Christ my Lord does all things well, Been down in-to de sea.

It is interesting that although the words of the sailor chantey, the *Mariner's Hymn*, and the spiritual are different they have a salt-water connection.

The spiritual *Who'll Jine de Union* is closely related in both words and music to a white song, *The Christian Band*, published in *Millennial Harp*. The white tune goes as follows:

The spiritual is as follows:

The spiritual improves melodically and rhythmically on the white song, but is derived from it or from a variant of it.

Other instances cannot be given in detail here. To mention a few tunes briefly: The choruses of *Roll, Jordan, Roll* and *Lord, Remember Me* are borrowed from Stephen Foster's *Camptown Races*; *I'm a Rollin' Through an Unfriendly Worl'* is based upon a white hymn, *Judgment*; *Old Ship of Zion* was taken over in whole from a white song of the same name; *There's a Meeting Here Tonight* was derived from the tune of *My Brother, I Wish You Well*; *Ride on, Jesus* is related to a white song of the same name; *De Angel Rolled de Stone Away* is derived from the opening phrase of the tune of Gibbon's old hymn beginning "Angels! roll the rock away," and *Swing Low, Sweet*

Chariot shows a relation, with striking rhythmic changes, to a tune of *Amazing Grace*.

Some idea of the extent of borrowing is seen in the fact that, of eighty-two tunes in one white song book, *Millennial Harp*, eleven are found in whole or in part in Negro spirituals, and this book is by no means confined to the folksy type of white religious songs. Various types of borrowing are represented: (1) both tune and words borrowed with very little alteration, (2) tune alone borrowed and melodic and rhythmic adaptations made by Negroes, (3) short phrase of white tune used as basis for a spiritual tune, with characteristic rhythmic alterations.

While the number of spirituals thus traced back to white tunes is still relatively small, it seems certain that, in view of the established fact that some of the best spirituals were borrowed, the more this subject is investigated the greater will appear the indebtedness of the spiritual to white religious folk songs.

St. Helena Island furnishes an important point in the argument. Of the eleven tunes mentioned as traceable to the tunes in one white book alone, ten are sung on St. Helena Island. This tends to confirm the theory that the spirituals took their origin in the upper South during the white camp-meeting movement and that their migration has been generally from North to South. The spirituals now sung in the out-of-the-way places like St. Helena are not, therefore, indigenous spirituals, but are for the most part the surviving remnants of the earlier spirituals.

To claim that the Negro took all of the spirituals from white tunes, that he has contributed nothing himself, would be stupid. There are undoubtedly spirituals of Negro composition, there are some white songs of Negro origin, and there are probably a few tunes which came from Africa. Furthermore, the instances of borrowing nearly all show that Negroes made rhythmic changes in the tunes they borrowed. Syncopation is the soul of African rhythms, likewise of the rhythms of spirituals, and since this trait is not pronounced in white folk music, it is probably a survival from African music.

But, if the several possible theories concerning the spirituals be listed as follows: (1) they are derived directly from Africa, (2) they are of American Negro origin, based on African patterns, (3) they are selections from white music, selections influenced by the Negro's African musical heritage, (4) they are largely borrowed directly from white folk music, as attested by the presence of the same traits to about the same extent in both musics; then it is seen that either of the latter two theories is more plausible than the former two.

There has been so much sentimentalizing on the spirituals that it will be difficult for some people to accept such a conclusion. The various statements of the "romantic" origins of the spirituals, of their being "America's only indigenous folk song," of their springing "ready made from the white heat of religious fervor," may be interesting as sentiments, but as scientific points of view on a question of musical relationships they are worthless. It is to be hoped that those who are convinced of the African origin of the spirituals will look closely into their English-American background before they embrace their conclusions.

After all, a question of musical relationships is unim-

ST. HELENA SONGS AND STORIES 73

portant from the point of view of art or appreciation. It would be foolish for anyone to love the spirituals any the less merely because they are shown to have more of a white past than has been supposed. Regardless of any "white man in the woodpile" in days past, these songs have come to represent in a real way the religious feelings and artistic expression of the American Negro. They are his own.

In the Sea Islands one may hear stories and superstitions that are rooted in the far distant childhood of the human race, folklore from Africa, Asia, Spain, England, and other parts of the globe. Story-telling is not a lost art with the Negroes. A stranger may have some difficulty in getting them started, but after he has lived among them for a while he meets with immediate response to any request for stories, riddles, "toasts," and the like.

In her book, *Folklore of the Sea Islands, South Carolina*, Elsie Clews Parsons has brought together nearly two hundred stories, numerous riddles, proverbs, rhymes, etc., the majority of which were collected on St. Helena Island. This work may be consulted for detailed information.

The folk stories of St. Helena represent several different types of heritages. Undoubtedly the majority of the stories were brought there by Negroes, but not all of them are native African stories. Some appear to have been carried from the Iberian Peninsula or from the Cape Verde Islands by sailors to West Africa, whence they were brought by the Negroes to the United States. Others are of Asiatic descent, having been taken into Africa long before the slave trade began. Still others were European tales learned by the Negroes in the West Indies and brought by them into the Southern States when they were sold to the early planters on the Carolina and Georgia coast. Added to these are European tales brought over by the English settlers or imported more recently by other Europeans. The culture of the sea island Negroes is, therefore, singularly rich in folk stories.

There is a close kinship, not only in type of story and subject matter, but in dialect and idiom, between the St. Helena tales and the folk stories told by the Negroes of the Bahamas. The relationship is not accidental, for there was a cross-migration between the Bahamas and the Southern colonies. West Indian and other island planters are known to have moved to South Carolina and Georgia, bringing slaves with them, and in the early plantation days in these colonies the planters preferred the seasoned slaves of the West Indies over the raw Africans. On the other hand, the turn of political events in the American colonies caused some, particularly the United Loyalists, to move to the Bahamas and other islands, taking their households with them.

An example of kinship is found in the habit of opening a story with

> Once upon a time, a wery good time,
> Monkey chaw tobacco an' spit white lime,

or

> Monkey chaw tobacco an' goose drink wine,

or some other variant of this rhyme, which is found on St. Helena as well as in the Bahamas. Mrs. Parsons said of this opening, "There was no trace in the Carolina tales," but the present writer found its use to be rather common,

ST. HELENA SONGS AND STORIES 75

especially on Ladies Island, adjoining St. Helena. It is one of those things which is stored in memory and is not used unless some train of association sets it off. A group of boys were telling stories. All of a sudden, one of them recalled this old nominee and began his story with it. Immediately the others wanted to give their versions of it, and in less than a minute seven or eight variations of this opening rhyme had been contributed.

There are also many points of similarity between the sea island tales and the African folk stories. The hare or rabbit, an important animal in the folklore of many peoples, plays the same rôle in the African tales that he does in the sea island tales. He nearly always outwits the other animals by his cunning, deceit, and trickery. No one could read works like Chatelain's *Folk Tales of Angola*, Dennett's *Folk-lore of the Fjort* (French Congo), or Nassau's *Where Animals Talk*, without concluding that a great many of the African tales have come into our country with very little change except that which was necessitated by the adaptation to English culture.

The charm of the stories told by the Negroes lies more in the way they are told than in the stories themselves. As Mrs. Parsons has said, "The characteristic emphasis of Negro tales, the drawl, and the tricks of speeding up, are difficult to indicate on paper. Italics and exclamation points are but feeble indicators; and how can one express by printers' signs the significance of what is *not* said?— a significance conveyed by manner or by quietness of intonation, of which a good story-teller is past master." Stripped of the tricks of the story-teller and of the dialect in which they are told, and written down in good English, these tales are apt to lose much of their flavor.

To the student of folklore, this vast body of stories is something to be collected, preserved, studied, compared, analyzed, something which it would be a shame to let die out. But to the Negroes these stories are like any other stories. They lie tucked away in memory most of the time. Occasionally they are called forth to do their bit toward entertaining the teller and his listeners. New stories, perhaps cheap stories, are constantly crowding in upon them, and if some of the old-time ones which go back almost to Adam slip out of memory through disuse, no tears are shed. Finding a rare tale may thrill the collector, but the Islanders may think something else is far more valuable. To them a story of a stuttering slave's being beaten up by a stuttering Irish patrol, because the Irishman thought the Negro was mocking him, may be much more attractive than Buh Rabbit's victory over Buh Lion.

The folklorist may complain that the art of story-telling is dying, but he must admit that the wonderful old stories are safe for some time yet among the Negroes of the Sea Islands. The older people rarely tell the stories to white people, it is true, but the children tell them naïvely and with plenty of skill. On the way to school, at recess time, at parties, at home around the fireside, or at work, the young folk tell stories and riddles. They may deviate from the traditional version of a tale, but they are good at supplying new incidents and at combining several stories to make a new one. If part of a story is supposed to be sung, they sing it rather than recite it as many adults would do.

If Buh Rabbit is supposed to make a funny noise as he runs down the road, this is supplied with an ingenuity which attempts to outdo the other fellow.

Several hundred riddles are in circulation among the Negroes on St. Helena. The children can recall an amazing number of them, especially if a contest is held to determine who knows the most riddles. Some of them will even make up new ones on the spot in order to keep in the game. The following riddles are among those heard most frequently:

1. Horse in de stable an' reinge [reins] outside, or Horse in de stable an' mange [mane] outside.—*Ans.:* 'Tatuh in de bed an' wine [vine] outside.
2. Chip cherry up, chip cherry down, No man can climb chip cherry tree.—*Ans.:* Smoke.
3. Black hen set on de red hen nes'.—*Ans.:* Pot on de fiah.
4. Somet'in' run all day an' all night an' nevah stop runnin'.— *Ans.:* Tide. (Also clock, wind, river.)

For the most part the riddles seem to be of European descent, although in some instances it is difficult to say whether a riddle is African or European. A few of them sound more like the African figurative discussions than the ordinary English riddle, as for example,

A rose in de gyaa'den an' a rose outside. What one you take? —*Ans.:* Rose in de gyaa'den is married gal, rose outside unmarried gal.

In general, it may be said that the folk beliefs of the St. Helena people are not different from the beliefs of the Southern Negroes as a whole. Indeed, they have actually ceased to take seriously many of the old-time beliefs and practises because of the influence which Penn School has had. Undoubtedly there are still people who patronize "root-doctors" or "conjuh men" in order to get "charms" or to cast "spells" on their enemies, there are some who actually use the folk remedies for various ills, and there are some who plant crops and kill hogs according to lunar phases, but the general status of the island culture as far as superstition is concerned is not very far below the level of the more backward white groups in this country.

Following are some of the superstitions which are actually practised to some extent. Midwives sometimes put a hoe or plow point or an axe under the bed to cut the after-pains of child-birth. It is also thought that if the patient will drink tea made from gizzard which has been dried and powdered, or tea made from the nest of the mud dauber, the after-pains will be reduced. Most families try to pay the midwife promptly for her services, for it is believed that failure to pay may cause her eyes, or even her mind, to be affected. Sometimes a Bible or a broom may be seen lying on the pillow above the head of a sick person. This is supposed to prevent the spirits from taking the person away. Mrs. King, the community nurse, stated that she has occasionally had to combat the use of such remedies as cow excreta and vinegar heated for boils, brown pea liquor as a wash for smallpox, a mixture of lard and mocking-bird bush (cassina) as an ointment for smallpox, soot for cuts, and lemon juice and ashes for colds.

One woman reproved a member of the research staff because he threw away two rats which had been killed in a trap. She said that the rats were just the thing she needed for a tea which she wanted to brew for her ten-year-old son to cure him of bed-wetting. The same woman believed that her failure to "bind" the boy—that is, to wrap cloth tightly around his abdomen—while he was a baby had resulted in his being weak physically. Another woman believed that if a stammering child drank water from a bell he would be cured.

Many mothers with babes in arms will call the baby's spirit when they start home after a visit, believing that the spirit might stay behind and evil consequences ensue unless it is called. It is considered bad luck to let a baby be near the coffin at a funeral. If one is present he is passed over the coffin from one person to another in order to prevent his spirit from accompanying the dead. A teacher at Penn School said that on one occasion his infant was taken to a funeral. He had thought nothing of the superstition, but other people at the funeral became very much disturbed on seeing the baby and would give him no peace until he had passed the child across the coffin.

As elsewhere in the South, the St. Helena people put the things last used and most prized by a person upon his grave. These are usually china, glasses, pitchers, medicine bottles, and other inexpensive things, but sometimes articles of value are left on the graves—antique clocks, vases, and the like. Most families still cover up all mirrors and stop the clocks in the house for a time after a death. An old woman pointed out some spots on a mirror, saying that the spots were eyes of spirits which came back because the mirror was not covered. The water used to bathe the dead person must be disposed of carefully, for to step over the place where it is poured will cause boils and sores on the legs.

Looking at the folk culture of St. Helena in a broad way, one is led to the conclusion that the outstanding thing about it is the way in which geographical and cultural isolation have made for the survival of old culture patterns, both European and African. Perhaps the next most striking thing is the predominance of the English culture over the African, as exemplified in dialect survivals, folk songs, superstitions, social and religious customs. Those who think of the Sea Islands as the reservoir *par excellence* of African culture traits are both right and wrong. The segment of Negro culture which comes nearest to being a replica of African culture is found in the animal tales, and these are, of course, found in a better state of preservation in the Sea Islands than anywhere else in this country. But, at the same time, the sea island folk furnish us with about as good a replica of 17th and 18th century peasant English culture as could be found in this country. There is no paradox here. Like any other subordinate group in a carefully disciplined slave régime such as existed in the South, the Negro tended to substitute the culture of the dominant race for his own culture. In this instance the process was accelerated by the religious views of the white evangelists, views which tabooed many items of Negro culture, such as native music, religious dances, voodooism, in fact, practically everything except the animal stories, which, although they were secular, were a source of pleasure to the white people and were therefore encouraged.

ST. HELENA SONGS AND STORIES

Those who believe in the unchangeableness of human nature in general, and in the racial inferiority of the Negro in particular, might do well to ponder upon the Negroes of St. Helena Island, who, in adapting themselves to our culture, have taken on the social and mental traits which accompany the borrowed culture. Relative to the time and place which they occupy in the scheme of things, they have adjusted themselves to the conditions of life and to one another with the minimum of social and personal disorganization.

CHAPTER IV

THE PEOPLE

And I shall not,
Shall not be removed.
And I shall not,
Shall not be removed.
Just like a tree
That's planted by the water,
And I shall not be removed.

St. Helena has always been predominantly Negro with about one hundred white residents. In 1920 there were over five thousand Negroes in this black rural community.[1] The few white residents, in ante-bellum times, were the planters and their overseers. The planters lived on the Island for only a few months in the year. Since the Civil War the whites have been engaged largely in merchandizing and operating oyster canneries, with a scattering few in farming. This unusually heavy proportion of blacks has come about because the island plantations had unusually large numbers of slaves, and here the descendants of slaves

[1] In 1850 there were only 250 whites to 7,600 Negroes in St. Helena Parish. The Parish then included Port Royal Island with the town of Beaufort as well as the present township. In 1920 there were 5,050 Negroes and 108 whites on St. Helena and Ladies Island.

The population discussed in this chapter refers to the whole of St. Helena Township including Ladies Island with 970 people in 1928, Coosaw with 186, Wassaw with 144 and St. Helena and immediately adjacent islands with 3,365.

THE PEOPLE 83

have stayed while many of the owners' families have moved.

The area has depended entirely upon natural excess of births over deaths for its increase. The number of outsiders coming in has been negligible. It is an inbred community, getting its few outside contacts from those who fare forth and return. Isolation has left the present population about as pure in Negro blood as could be found. There is now no intermixture with whites and there was little in ante-bellum days. The few mulattoes who resulted from these early matings have long since gone, leaving the pure blacks.

From 1860 [2] there was a uniform increase in number of Negroes up to 1900, but since 1900 there has been a sharp decrease. In recent years the decrease has noticeably slackened. As will appear later this shrinkage in population comes largely through economic forces over which the people had little control.

It is interesting to note that while the culture of sea island cotton was profitable, the township under a system of free farming supported more people than it did under the slave system. For forty years after freedom the natural increase was steady. They were busy begetting.

It is evident that the growth in population was due to a very heavy excess of births over deaths, as immigration into the Island has been so negligible that the few outsiders were very conspicuous. It is not at all unusual to see older women who have borne more than ten children. One is "mother of twenty-five, grandmother of fifty-two

[2] See Table I, Statistical Information. All tables are in this section, pp. 261-262.

and great grand- of nine head of children." The 1910 census counted the number of dead and living children, born to each mother, and the results of this table are given in Table XXII. It is astonishing to see that 306 or more than one-fourth had had over ten children and 402 had had between five and ten children. This tremendous fertility of the Negroes, not in the Sea Islands alone, but throughout the rural districts of the South, has supplied the increase in the farming population and sent many to swell the tide flowing into the cities. The cities barely maintain themselves by the balance of births and deaths and their increase comes from the country.

The present size of St. Helena families, five living members as against six members in 1910, indicates that this fertility is decreasing. In the present shrinking population, the excess of births over deaths is smaller than it was formerly, and there is an outward movement as well. For the eight years, 1920 to 1927, there were 1,170 births and 735 deaths, an excess of fifty-four per year. This provides an annual increase in the population of 11.2 per thousand, which compares favorably with the increase of Negroes in the United States as a whole. In 1924 the natural increase for the total Negro population was 3.3 per thousand in cities [3] and 11.7 in rural districts.

The reduction of population since 1900 is sufficiently drastic to raise a question as to the future of the community if present tendencies continue. For the individuals concerned, this upheaval represents hundreds of decisions to break the ties of land and family and seek strange places. In common with other rural sections of the South, St.

---

[3] Cities of over ten thousand population.

Helena Island has been losing in population for about thirty years. Here is written the result of the gradual depression of agriculture in the South.

The interesting feature of this migration has been that it was more rapid before the advent of the boll weevil than it has been since the boll weevil disorganized sea island cotton. The boll weevil arrived on the Island in effective numbers in 1918 and, therefore, did not seriously affect the movement of population before the census of 1920. However, for two decades before that, the population had been shrinking. The fact that the people are constantly leaving this farm community, which, in many respects, is as favorable a situation for Negroes as can be found anywhere in the rural South, is a danger signal for the Negro in agriculture.

General studies of Negro migration have emphasized several factors as causes of the movement: poor schools; unsatisfactory race relationships, especially in the dealings between the landlord and tenant; and in some communities, violence and actual disregard for civil rights and bodily safety of Negro citizens. None of these, however, operate on St. Helena Island. While the public schools are poorer than those of the city, they are near the average of Southern rural Negro schools and they are supplemented by private instruction in Penn School which cannot be surpassed in any Negro educational institution of its scope in the country. There have been so few white people in the section and the interests of these have been so closely allied with the interest of the colored people that the relationship between the races has been most satisfactory and there have been no opportunities for violence or reason for injustice, except in the indirect acts of the county government in apportioning public funds to St. Helena Township. As the Negroes have all been landowners, the difficulties of the tenant system have not entered into the picture.

It is necessary to search farther into the situation for the causes of this movement. Some of the elements are made clear in the discussion of the condition of agriculture, from which it is apparent that the presence of the boll weevil is not the only unfavorable factor to be considered, but that the people are facing other discouraging situations.

From 1885 to 1894 phosphate mining was a thriving industry in the county. Many men from the Island as well as from the mainland were employed. A few of the older inhabitants estimate that these companies employed about one thousand Negroes, most of whom were from St. Helena and Ladies Islands. The Coosaw Mining Company alone operated four big boats in the extraction phase of their industry. With each tug boat was a dredge and a wash boat. Ten men usually went on the dredges and ten on the wash boats. Each boat was also usually followed closely by one or two small boats, each containing two men. The function of the men in these small boats was to pick up the pieces of rock missed by the dredge. It is said that when the water was too deep to allow a man to wade alongside the boat he would dive to the bottom, pick up a piece of the phosphate bearing rock, come to the top of the water long enough to deposit his finding in the boat, catch his breath, and dive again like a duck.

In 1893, acting under the recommendation of Governor

THE PEOPLE

Tillman, the legislature of South Carolina levied a royalty of one dollar per ton on the phosphatic rock mined from the rivers. The smaller companies tried in vain to compensate for the royalties by cutting wages of the "divers," or hand pickers. The result was, that by 1898 there were no hand pickers. The Brotherhood Mine ceased operation in 1893. Later in the same year the Pacific Mining Company succumbed. In 1894 the Sea Island Company sold out to the Coosaw Mining Company and the Coosaw moved its whole plant, in 1894, to Ship Yard Point.

Concomitant with the royalty came the destructive hurricane of 1893. Dredges were destroyed, lighters were carried away, and small boats were lost or destroyed. The storm was largely responsible for the Coosaw Mining Company moving its operation base. By 1894, phosphate mining on a large scale in Beaufort County was a thing of the past.

In 1898 competition from Florida was becoming very keen. The South Carolina rock bore about 55 per cent phosphoric acid. That discovered in Florida was not only of a higher percentage but could be mined more economically because of the absence of the expense of water dredging, washing and drying processes, and the absence of a heavy royalty. In 1904 the Coosaw Mining Company went out of business in Beaufort. The Central lasted until 1906.

According to a few of the older inhabitants of Beaufort, the phosphate industries had furnished many of the Island Negroes their sole opportunity for earning a little cash money. With the decline of the industry, not only were those who were directly employed by the industries deprived of employment but also many Negroes who were furnished boats by Beaufort speculators to pick phosphates on shares. Some of the Negroes owned their own boats and sold their small pickings to the companies for $1.25 per ton. Undoubtedly the 1900-1910 migration was partly an aftermath of the decline of this industry.

There is another political-economic situation which probably augmented the migration from 1900-1910. In 1894 a dry-dock was built at Parris Island. The size of the dock and the economic importance of having such a dock can be ascertained when it is considered that the Battleship *Indiana* was docked there. Many island Negroes were employed. Unfortunately, however, the dock was built of wood. Being exposed to the broiling sun six months out of the year, and continuously to the salt water, it soon began to warp and to rot. When the agitation in 1898 was started to have the wooden dock replaced by a concrete structure, a delegation persuaded Congress to have the dry-dock moved to Charleston and this source of local revenue was also lost. Considering the heavy movement which followed the breakdown of the phosphate industry and the 1893 and 1911 hurricanes, it is remarkable that the loss of population between 1920 and 1928 was only about 7 per cent.

It should be emphasized, however, that loss of population is a condition which is not peculiar to St. Helena Island or to the Negro in general, but is only an epitome of the general shift from country to city by all population groups in the United States and as such it deserves as careful an

THE PEOPLE 89

analysis and as accurate a description as can be made in order to throw light upon the general problem.

When the movement from St. Helena is compared to the movement from some of the other Southern rural areas, it is apparent that the holding power of landownership, good schools, and the opportunity to supplement farm income with day labor have minimized the displacement of population. If St. Helena is compared with Greene County, Georgia, which represents the disorganized tenant area of the Georgia Black Belt, it is evident that the movement from St. Helena has been far less since the advent of the boll weevil.

An examination of the decrease in the different parts of the Island, 1920 to 1928, as shown by Table III, indicates that the decreases have been greatest in the outlying portions of the Island on more isolated peninsulas where the opportunity for supplementing farm income with wages is less than on the central portions.

While the central portion gained about 4 per cent in population the outlying section lost about 16 per cent. Coffin Point and Fripp Point, the heaviest losers, are approximately six miles from the nearest wage-earning opportunity with the exception of a small truck farm on Coffin Point. Coosaw and Wassaw Islands are inaccessible on account of intervening tide rivers, and only a portion of the lower end of St. Helena Island is convenient by water transport to Parris Island.

This is a reversal of the usual tendency for migration to be greatest where the communication with cities is easiest. In fact, the population of Ladies Island, which is closest to the mainland, actually shows a slight increase.

In other words, there are two types of communities in the township; one where isolation from other sections throws the people back largely on farming, and the other where farming is supplemented by day labor on neighboring large truck farms, in the oyster canneries, or at Parris Island Marine Base. The holding power of these non-agricultural opportunities in rural districts is similar to that which has been observed in other rural sections, such as portions of the piedmont area of North Carolina and South Carolina, where the families who are still living on the land spend part of their time working in near-by cotton mills thus stabilizing their income to a greater degree than if they were dependent entirely upon the products of the farm.

The effects of this movement upon the composition of the population remaining are fundamental. It has already been noted that one of the first effects is the reduction of the birth rate by the draining off of people of child-bearing age. This is evident in the sharp reduction of the number of island children under ten years of age between 1910 and 1928 (from 1,700 in 1910 to 900 in 1928). This reduction is due in part to migrant families who carry their children with them but more to the movement of women of child-bearing age. From Table IV it would seem that about three hundred women of child-bearing age are among the migrants. Here we have a clear picture of how migration has reduced the tremendous fertility of the Negro rural population. It has carried the young people away, leaving the old, thus reducing the number who would have been born.

THE PEOPLE

Migration has also caused an unbalanced sex and age distribution in the population. (Table IV.) Old people and women form a disproportionate number of those left behind. One of the most important results of this distortion of the population by migration is apparent in the fact that about one-third of the families are headed by widows, many of whom, though advanced in years, are caring for several young grandchildren or grandnieces and nephews, while the intermediate generation has migrated to the city. These old people have a hard struggle against nature to eke out a bare subsistence and the lives of the children in their custody are circumscribed a great deal.

The lives of these widows is typified by one of our neighbors. She is seventy-four and no longer able to pursue her profession as midwife, or to engage in active work in the field. From time to time she shoulders her heavy hoe and ties up her hips with heavy cord to "gib stren'th" and does what she can. Through the migration of her daughter to Savannah, she has acquired four grandchildren to care for. The children are able to do some light work in the gathering of compost and cultivation of the crops, but there is no one to do the heavy plowing or hoeing. The land is unfenced so that the animals have to be staked out to forage and constantly watched. All of the children are visibly undernourished and it was quite an experiment at the headquarters of the study to try to fill them up with food and to see how much would be required. Incredible quantities were eaten. When she was asked in the early spring what she had on hand in way of food she said, "Few peas and some cracked corn."

Another widow was found who had only one acre of

land, but was keeping a calf, a cow, several pigs, and a number of chickens and turkeys. It was evident that her animals were foraging on the neighborhood and inasmuch as she was living alone, she probably was not suffering for want of food.

Miss Cooley [4] had the following account of the straits of one of these old women written down as recounted to the island merchant:

"'Mr. Mac, I too glad fo' look 'pon yo' face once mo'!'

"'Yes, Aunt Jane, I'm very glad to see you too. How are you, and how are you getting along?'

"'Poo-el-ly, Mr. Mac, poo-el-ly. Ain't you see how I cripple! Dis ain't de Jane you use-tuh know. My whole frame is weak, and ax for my knee, I wouldn't talk, it's so painful. You know, Mr. Mac, when Jane Rivers fetch little bit o' cotton like to dat, times mus' be change. Mr. Mac, I couldn't tell you how I struggle to make dat one bag full o' cotton. I jus' try for plant a tas' [¼ acre], and dat'll tell you how far back I gone. You members when Jane been a *Jane*, two acres wuz play for me. I go out to de cotton patch in de mornin', stick in one han', and hoe in de udder. I jus' try fer hoe two row. I hoe an' I hop, an' I hoe an' I hop. Presently here comes de misery in me knee, an' it hu't me so bad I bleeged to fall in de alley on me back. An', Mr. Mac, turn and twis' as I will, I cyan' rise up. De is so bad I cry. I hab to cry, Mr. Mac. I cry wid de pain, and I cry wid de agrawation. I say, "Do, Jesus, he'p dis poor old 'ooman in de misery!" I whoop so dem people could hear me and come he'p me, an' get back to de house. When I ketch me bret I say,

[4] Cooley, *Homes of the Freed*, pp. 93-96.

"Sue, do kindle fire and pit pot on so I kin cook hominy and get strenk to try again." . . . ' "

These old widows head a good proportion of the families. Some are not in such reduced circumstances, in fact one or two more vigorous widows are in the successful farmer group.

By questioning the heads of families as to the location of absent members of the family, 1,610 migrants are accounted for. Of these, 1,113 have migrated since 1920 and 497 had migrated before 1920. The deaths among the earlier migrants, of course, have reduced this number considerably below the number of members of these families which have actually moved.

This list was supplemented by a check of the families present in the 1920 census and absent in the 1928 enumeration. From this source it was possible to account for 73 families including the 195 individuals. It was not possible to secure the destination of these family migrants as it was not known with sufficient accuracy. However, it is reasonable to presume it was distributed in about the same way as the individual movement.

The question naturally arises as to what becomes of the people when they leave home and go to the cities. What of their new economic and social status?

Even among a group of people who come from families of fairly uniform economic status and educational opportunities, differences in individual ability and initiative are so great that it is difficult to compare the status of the migrants in cities and their former status on the Island. Another difficulty is that many who leave are just beginning to work and hence have no island background of employment. There are too many changing conditions to be able to state, in individual cases, whether the migrant has bettered his condition or not. Who can say, for instance, how much the high wages received in cities should be discounted to compensate for the fresh air and easy food supply of St. Helena? Who can say how much the presence of mosquitoes on the Island should be debited to the Island and how much the noise of the cities should be debited to the cities? How much are the community agencies and institutions worth to the individual on the Island and what about the dens of vice in a city? At best the question can be disposed of only by individual reactions.

Amid the diversities of personal reactions from migrants encountered in the cities, two prominent characteristics stand out almost universally, especially among the more recent migrants. The first is that the pull of the city has been a cause of migration as strong as the push forces of the Island. The second is that there is little desire to return to the old home, as long as the present handicaps of agriculture and relatively steady city employment continue. Many expressed a wish to return if more money could be made. The large proportion of migrants have not yet been subjected to a prolonged industrial depression. Their attitude under such conditions would be problematical.

The following statement by a migrant is given because it sums up so well the apparent reason why so many young people have deserted their homes. It shows how they rationalize their move.

THE PEOPLE

"The people had been livin' in the dark. They didn't know they was in reach of any place other than the cotton field. Then, when the war broke out and soldiers were carried away, they saw how easy it was to travel. They naturally would not be content to go back to the country to spend their days. Their eyes were opened. They tasted something better. They wrote to their friends after they came to New York, and *opened their* eyes so the people began coming. When *they* get here and stay awhile, maybe *they* have a relative or friend that wants to come up. So they send *him* money."

The families of the Island report that of their missing members 50 per cent are in Savannah, 25 per cent are in New York, and 25 per cent in miscellaneous Northern and Southern cities. Subsequent checks in these cities, however, reveal that quite a number have moved on from Savannah to the North without keeping in touch with relatives so that at present probably 40 per cent are in Savannah and 30 per cent in New York with 20 per cent in miscellaneous Northern cities and 10 per cent in miscellaneous Southern cities. The actual numbers are about 480 in New York as compared with the 600 in Savannah, about 100 in Philadelphia and 50 in Boston and practically 75 in Charleston. There are some 200 well scattered in other Northern and Southern cities.

A striking feature of this movement is the negligible number who report their destination as Beaufort, a small town which is only eleven miles from the center of the Island, and the small number going to Charleston, only eighty miles away. The limited opportunities for employment in these towns evidently do not offer inducement in any way comparable to the opportunities in Savannah and New York.

Though none of the migrants save much after the high rents have been paid, those in New York, Philadelphia and Boston have a higher standard of living than do the bulk of those in Savannah or Charleston. The explanation is that more of the northern male migrants were in skilled labor or professions than in Savannah, where the large majority are stevedores or unskilled laborers. The average wage earner in New York works regularly as clockwork and must be as punctual if he holds his job. The St. Helena male laborers in New York earn about $20 per week as compared with $10 in Savannah. In Savannah the women doing housework get about $6 per week and their meals. In New York the women are paid around $16 per week without meals for eight hours of work per day. A few are able to find casual employment at the rate of 40 to 50 cents per hour.

Savannah is only seventy-five miles by water from St. Helena, and the trip costs only seventy-five cents. Thus Savannah, a city of some 112,000, has long been the most familiar city to the Islanders, a place to which hundreds of visitors and floating laborers go and return during the slack seasons on the farm. This is the first loosening of home ties and practically all migrants, no matter what their final destination, pass through the Savannah stage.

The bulk of the migrants in Savannah from St. Helena Island have settled in two compact areas near the Savannah River. These two sections are the *Fort* on the east side, and the *Yemacraw* on the west side. The rent paid in these two sections is about ten dollars per month [5] for three rooms. This is about two dollars cheaper than rentals in better Negro districts farther north from the River. The rent appears to be small enough, but considering the fact that the weekly wages of the inhabitants of these areas rarely exceed ten dollars, it is understood that this is an excessive proportion to be spent for rent.

This tendency of the newcomers to gravitate to these two sections may be explained by comparatively low rents, the clannish nature of the people, and by the proximity to the wharves and to the factories near the wharves. A few, however, have managed to emerge from these poor sections and are buying homes out on Henry Street, a very good section.

Although Charleston is as near as Savannah, few migrants from St. Helena have gone there. This is due to the greater accessibility to Savannah and to better opportunities for finding work there. The few individuals who have gone to Charleston were found to be scattered among the many small Negro sections, living, for the most part, in rented flats or in small huts in one of Charleston's many extremely narrow "courts." Though the demand for stevedores is much less than in Savannah, the type of labor obtained by most of the male migrants is on a parity with that of Savannah so far as wages are concerned.

The Islanders in Philadelphia are well scattered over the city. There are many more scattered Negro neighborhoods in Philadelphia than there are in New York. Hence, there are no large central places of amusement there. For

---

[6] These rents are slightly below the average in Charleston which in 1925 was found to be $12.44 per month.

this reason, plus the presence of friends or relatives in New York, many St. Helena Negroes have taken the hop from Philadelphia to New York.

Over half of the migrants in Boston were found in the Roxbury section. More like a Negro section of Southern cities than Harlem does the quiet Roxbury section appear with its numerous low apartment buildings and frame tenement houses. The others were scattered in surrounding suburbs such as Medford, West Medford, Lynn, West Lynn, and Everett. A fair proportion of those living in the suburbs owned their homes.

Most of these in Boston were over thirty years of age and had been there for ten years or more. Few of the recent migrants go there. The recent tide is to New York.

In New York, about 375 Islanders were in Harlem, 50 in Brooklyn, 25 in Columbus Hill, 15 in Corona, Long Island, and a few scattered through the city.

Of the 86 men interviewed in New York, 50 were unskilled laborers, 13 skilled, 15 were clerical workers, 2 were of school age, 3 were professional men, 1 was leader of a "numbers" ring, 1 was pensioned, and one able-bodied man was unemployed.

Of the 135 women interviewed, 82 were doing housework outside the home. Twenty-two reported that they simply worked at keeping their own home. The others reported miscellaneous jobs.

The homes in New York range from the best to the worst —from those of two families gradually buying their homes in the new Dunbar Apartments to dives of filth in Columbus Hill and Harlem. A small proportion is found in these extremes. The majority are in the middle range.

THE PEOPLE 99

There is no doubt that the few in the upper levels of employment have bettered themselves considerably by leaving the Island. This group includes, besides the three professional men, some of the skilled laborers and a few of the clerical workers. The postoffice employees, for instance, draw salaries ranging around $2,100 and $2,300, and have practical assurance of a lifetime job with a pension. Those in casual unskilled labor would probably be as well off on the Island. Their homes in New York are squalid and their work is poorly paid and uncertain. Though practically all in these classes were managing to get along, a stretch of acute unemployment conditions in the city would quickly strike them to the bone and render them dependent upon charity. Among the steadier unskilled laborers and domestics the individuals have in many cases, victrolas, pianos, and radios. Though they enjoy higher standards of living, few report being able to save any money after expenses are paid.

The lack of budgets of St. Helena families living in cities makes it impossible to compare statistically the incomes of these families with those on the Island. The reports of the bulk of the migrants in New York, however, indicate that after the necessities are bought little is left.[6] So, irrespective of the somewhat higher standard of living and chances for commercialized recreation in New York, and irrespective of the values inherent in the simple life of St. Helena, there is a question as to whether

[6] In Harlem the average five-room apartment furnishing steam heat and hot water rents for $60 per month. Single rooms in this type of building usually bring $5 per week. "Cold water flats" in Harlem bring about $40 per month and the same type usually rents for $30 in Brooklyn or Columbus Hill.

there is much difference of "real wages" between the bulk of migrants and the St. Helena inhabitants. In order to approximate the standard maintained by the island families with an average income of $420 conservatively figured, city laborers would have to earn about $20 per week or $1,000 per year to compensate for higher rent and food costs in Northern cities.

The contrast of the monotony of life on St. Helena, with many commercialized forms of recreation in New York, was cited by many of the younger people as being their reason for leaving and the reason why they do not care to return. "Nothin' to do in that dead place." "I'd be scared to go live in them dark snaky places." "Down on the Island it's the same thing over and over every day. You get up in the morning, milk the cows, eat breakfast, go out and work all day, come in and eat. Then it gets dark and you go to bed. You get up the next morning and do the same thing over and over again. Sunday comes, of course, and you go to church. Everybody goes to church there. Then, of course, you have a few prayer meetings now and then, little parties and dances. I didn't know how monotonous it was while I was there, but after I got up here 'n' saw how, every night, people had so many different kinds of amusement, I began thinking. I wasn't in a hurry to go back home."

But in spite of the absence of desire to return to the Island, such an expression as, "I'd rather be a lamp post on Lenox Avenue than a whole plantation on St. Helena," was exceptional. The friendly attitude of the migrants toward their home background is represented not only by the rather frequent short visits to the Island but also by

THE PEOPLE 101

the universal desire to be buried on the Island and by the frequent expressions of vague desires to "spend my last days there." Many say that, "de eart' dat bears you lies mo' lightly on yo' bones."

Socially there are several striking features of the movement of Negroes which indicate that it temporarily disorganizes Negro life.

(1) The birth rate is drastically reduced in both country and city by reason of the draining off of young women and young men from the country and their later marriage and harder struggle in the city.

(2) While dangers of typhoid and malaria are escaped in the city the ravages of tuberculosis, pneumonia and infant diseases are greatly increased.

(3) There is little choice between school advantages on the Island and in the city, though Negroes moving from the other average rural communities obtain greatly superior educational advantages for their children.

(4) A completely new cycle of leisure-time activities is encountered, more varied, more stimulating, but more costly and more allied to vice and demoralization.

As long as families on the Island are large and the plots of land to be inherited are small, children of island families will continue to seek the city as they grow up. Which should stay and which should go will depend largely upon individual traits and the condition of agriculture. It is as unreasonable to expect every boy born in the country to have the aptitudes of a farmer as it is to expect every boy in the city to be a good business man. The foregoing summary of the visits to migrants in cities indicate that quite a number of Islanders are capable of securing good employment. However, the condition of the masses of the migrants who have remained unskilled laborers in the city is such that it seems a toss-up as to whether they lead a fuller life and have more surplus leisure as they are in the city or as they would have been in the country. The movement cityward is too recent a phenomenon to really judge what its full implication may be.

CHAPTER V

HEALTH

*There is a Balm in Gilead,
To make the wounded whole;
There is a Balm in Gilead,
To heal the sin-sick soul.*

The present good health and long life on St. Helena is a contradiction to the theory that the Negro in America is naturally a sickly individual. This state of health, however, has been a hard won attainment, an evolution from magic and herb doctors, through faith in patent medicines, to modern medical care. Each improvement has been carefully directed by Penn School through its nurse, who, with her midwife allies, has been the chief foe of superstition.

Owing to their economic value, the health of slaves was rather carefully attended by masters. Nevertheless, for both whites and Negroes, the pre-Civil War death rates were high. Some fragmentary evidence as to slave deaths indicates that the plantation death rate in the Sea Islands was around eighty per thousand as against the present rate of nineteen on St. Helena. The reader of epitaphs in old family burying grounds is depressed by the rows of small graves of children lost at an early age.

In addition to the ministration of the owners, herb doctors were resorted to, for they were found by the early workers interested in the health of the freedmen. Miss

Towne [1] speaks of a Dr. Jacobs, "a man who has poisoned enough people with his herbs and roots and magic, for his chief remedy with drugs is spells and incantations." Rat tea, washing in the outgoing tide, dried frogs, and other remedies were popular, and are still known to some of the older inhabitants. Superstitious practices of this nature are today even more authoritative in other Sea Islands. Julia Peterkin's charming accounts of such nostrums in *Black April* are not overdrawn for other parts of the seacoast.

Many planters who have observed their tenants closely come to have a certain faith in this procedure themselves. They will half laughingly say that they have seen the remedies work. They have seen the healing herb close wounds and the bitter tea allay fevers. Crude as many of the superstitions are, they doubtless have a twofold value. Many of them have some sort of a basis in experience. Before the true nature of malaria was known it was believed by both whites and Negroes that a proper safeguard was to keep out of the night air and close the house tight. This was effective though the safety came, not by avoiding the "miasmas," but by keeping off the anopheles mosquitoes. Another value of superstitious remedies arises from their psychological effect. Ignorant people, when they get the slightest ailment, are often demoralized by fear, so that reassurance, whether it comes in the form of an herb tea or the mild pills of a physician, does more to restore vigor than pharmacopœa.

These practices have yielded slowly and many of them still continue. The older people still believe that illnesses

---

[1] Holland, Rupert S., *Letters and Diary of Laura M. Towne*, p. 232.

are "put down" for them by some secret enemy, or that they have come from divine dispensation. A visit by Miss House of Penn School for friendly enquiry elicited this explanation from one old woman.[2]

"Hump, hump!" shaking her head, "dey is some illness come from God, and some come from man!"

"Do you think this sickness came from God?" asked Miss House.

The little room was dark, the little old woman lay on a very neat bed, well cared for, evidently, but quite weak. "No," she whispered, "no, no! Dish yuh sickness came from man!"

"Do you think someone wished some evil on you?"

"Yes," came back the expected answer in a whisper.

"Some one of your kin?"

"No," emphatically. "But I couldn't tell oonuh who it was. I always did work for myself, an' dey didn't like it. But I've had some good relief since Monday. I went to the colored doctor an' she gib me some medicine dat gib me good relief."

"Was it drinking medicine?"

"Yes, and something mo'! She pray wid me, an' I pray too. It is t'rough de Lord de relief done come." . . .

This fatalistic attitude toward health has probably helped and hindered in equal measure. It hindered those whose fears were too greatly aroused and helped those who refused to worry until symptons of illness actually appeared.

Following faith in herb doctors and superstitious rem-

[2] Cooley, Rossa B., *Homes of the Freed*, pp. 40, 41.

edies, came faith in patent medicines. Miss Cooley tells of a woman who, during her early visits to the sick, informed her that she had "drunk nine dollars and fifty cents wuth of medicine" taking a last bottle to "cool de pain." Only a step removed from faith in patent medicine was the habit of sending long distances to the doctor for "drinkin'" or "rubbin'" medicine and expecting the physician to make a long distance diagnosis. But these practices are now far less in vogue on St. Helena than in the surrounding areas. The younger generation is adopting American health standards.

Isolation has been favorable to the control of such diseases as tuberculosis and syphilis, diseases considered by many as characteristic of Negro groups. The interest of Penn School in health, and the long and effective efforts of the island nurse, have borne astounding fruits in raising the general health level. An especial achievement in the fundamentals of living is the reduction of infant mortality to a rate as low as the average of any state in the Union.

The general death rate of the Negroes on the Island compares favorably with other rural areas and is markedly better than in the cities. During the eight-year period from 1920 to 1928 the average annual death rate on St. Helena was 19.0 per thousand.[3] It was 20.4 per thousand for both white and colored in Beaufort County. The death rate of the Negroes in the whole registration area of the United

[3] The rate refined for age grouping is about the same as the crude rate since the normal Negro population has more children under 5 (tending to raise the rate) and fewer old people over 70 (tending to lower the rate). Table VII.

HEALTH

States in 1923 was 17.7 per thousand and that in cities was 22 per thousand.

This excess over the general rate for the whole country is due to the fact that malaria is present and accounts for enough deaths to make the difference between St. Helena and the general registration area.

Many of the former inhabitants of the Island who have settled in cities return to their relatives when fatally stricken with sickness. This desire to die at home also increases the death rate by reason of deaths within the community of ex-Islanders who are really non-residents.

A glance at the detailed causes of death, Table VIII, will dispel some striking pre-conceptions regarding Negro health and reveal some clean-cut advantages which the Islanders hold over their city neighbors. The principal differences in the causes of death are that pneumonia, tuberculosis, and infant mortality do not take nearly so great a toll of the population of the Island as they do from the Negro population in general. Tuberculosis ranks almost as high in the causes of death on St. Helena as in the whole Negro population, but it is the testimony of the doctor, nurse, and other well-informed people that every case of tuberculosis which has occurred on the Island for the past twenty years is traceable to outside infection. In other words, tuberculosis is not indigenous to the Island, but is brought in by people who move backward and forward to and from cities. Even so the rate of 168 per 100,000 on the Island is strikingly less than the rate in cities which is 300 per 100,000.[4] The disease is controlled by constant watchfulness of the doctor and nurse

---

[4] All cities in the registration area 1924.

in locating these returning cases and instructing the families in how to care for them so as to prevent infection of others. An official of the State Health Department found on a recent visit that all cases were properly cared for.

The contrast between the Island and the cities in pneumonia deaths is still greater. From this disease only 47 per 100,000 die on the Island as against 300 per 100,000 Negroes in the cities of the registration area. Infant mortality is also very much lower among these rural Negroes. In the Negro population of the cities of the whole registration area, there were 138 deaths of infants under one year of age for each 1,000 live births. In the combined Negro and white population of South Carolina, the infant death rate was 91 (1925)[5] and on St. Helena Island there were 48 deaths under one year per 1,000 births. (Eight-year average.) Very few states have an average loss of infants as low as this community. The deaths of women from child-birth are also below the usual figure, being only 28 per 100,000.

Another most favorable comparison is the fact that there are so many deaths from old age on the Island, whereas this cause is negligible in the city population. This is the sixth highest cause of mortality. A remarkable number of them are of an uncertain age. Judging from their vivid memory of slave days they are near ninety. This longevity is in itself a striking commentary on the health of the Island. Theirs is not a bedridden old age and seldom are they entirely dependent. Many of the old men and old women are straight as a string and do occasional field work or odd jobs up to the time of their last illness.

[5] The lowest rate in 5 years.

A BETTER HOME

MIDWIVES' CLASS

HEALTH

It is also a tribute to the sanitary work that typhoid is so rare as to account for about one death in two years, notwithstanding the fact that all the drinking water comes from shallow wells. On the other hand, the rates for malaria are much higher than in cities, though just about the same as in the rest of the low country area of South Carolina and not high enough to be alarming. The deaths from complaints of the digestive tract are greater than in the Negro population as a whole, owing to improper nourishment and lack of proper attention to digestion.

The most constant force in pressing public health measures is the work of Penn School and the nurse on the school staff who devotes her whole time to the Island. When the present principals came there was no doctor or nurse and the sick had to be carried to Beaufort or Parris Island for medical care, often waiting until they were almost dead before making this trip. Soon, however, a nurse was added to the school staff and the work has been continuous for over twenty years. Penn School has served as a demonstration center for community investigations of sanitation, hookworm, pellagra, tuberculosis and filaria.

The way in which these campaigns reach the people is described by Miss Cooley.[6] "An outbreak of typhoid fever one summer led us to organize our health campaign. There were twenty-two cases and five deaths, and we were faced with an epidemic." The State Department of Health sent a representative to map out a campaign which included inoculation and a propaganda for sanitary privies and driven wells. "The 'sanitaries' were simply wooden

[6] Cooley, Rossa B., *Homes of the Freed*, p. 51.

boxes, fly-proof, made according to a pattern that had been used in Virginia. A few made boxes for themselves, but most of them were made in the school carpenter shop at the cost of fifty-five cents. . . . One night I met Solomon carrying his box home from the shop on his head. . . . The next day I found, to my surprise, that he had planted his 'sanitary' squarely in front of his house. He greeted me proudly, 'Ain't she pretty?' "

Soon the district selected as a demonstration was 100 per cent perfect in the installation of "sanitaries" and driven wells. Very slowly from this demonstration plantation, where a special drive was made, the "sanitary" idea spread to other parts of the Island. Until now, as has been said before, typhoid is only an occasional rather than a constant menace.

Beaufort County also has the services of a full-time health officer and a public health nurse. A proportion of this work is done on St. Helena Island. The health officer comes over to attend to vaccinations and assist in the prevention of epidemics and the nurse cooperates in an occasional baby clinic and clinics for the diseases of children.

One of the Penn School graduates who has received medical training has returned to practice on the Island so that the people have a full-time physician also and they are gradually forming the habit of consulting him, although their decision to call him is often tardy.

The nurse has regular office hours for consultation as well as making regular rounds in the community. From five to ten people a day come in for help, ranging from pre-natal instruction to directions for care of tuberculosis patients and vaccination against communicable diseases.

HEALTH

Her work also includes regular examinations and inoculation of school children. Owing to the interest created in weights and measurements, twenty-seven children in a group of eighty were brought up to normal weight during the year 1928-29. She received over six hundred and fifty visits in the office and made over two hundred visits to the homes, touching almost nine hundred people during the year.

Probably the most effective public health measure and the one which accounts for the phenomenally low infant death rate and the small loss of mothers in child-birth has been the organization and instruction of the midwives. Midwifery has always held a definite status since plantation days. The slave-owners had the midwives carefully instructed and paid them a small fee for each case attended, with a bonus for each baby who survived the first year. Many of the secrets of their craft, however, were handed down by word of mouth and they included, in addition to the obstetrical instruction, a ritual of superstitious practice, one such practice which the nurse recently noted and which, according to African visitors to the Island, corresponds to African practice was to stand the woman in child-birth up in a corner and assist the process by having several robust women to beat, punch and shake her. Others which have been observed in the Sea Islands were to put a sharp axe under the bed to cut off the pains and to tie a piece of the umbilical cord around the toe of the mother for a relief after birth. Some of these women thought that it was injurious to bathe the baby before it was nine days old.

Miss Cooley's description of how this problem was initially attacked is contained in her little book, *The Homes of the Freed:* [7]

"Our nurse had given instruction to the women in the Community Class, but that reached only a few 'midders,' perhaps half a dozen. It seemed a bit casual to go on year after year with no birth or death records, so I had a set of cards printed and placed them in the hands of the doctor, the nurse, and each of the island ministers.

"The following year, South Carolina passed a law that all births and deaths must be recorded. Under the new law all midwives were compelled to register, and a course of twelve lessons was required in order to obtain a certificate to practice. Our school was used as a center, and the nurse appointed to give the course. We wondered how the women would like this new measure. We found great enthusiasm: forty-two enrolled at the first meeting. This includes Wassa, Ladies, and Palawanna Islands, as well as St. Helena. Twelve lessons only are required by the State, and yet for three years the midwives have come regularly to their monthly meeting, and not one is yet satisfied that she knows all that the 'Doctor Nuss' can pass on to her.

"I attended the first meeting. An interesting crowd had gathered, grandmothers of eighty, mothers from about fifty up. Some had come from Coffin's Point, some from Lands End, and every point of the Island and the near-by islands was represented. One note was struck that afternoon. The 'midders' work was recognized by the State; it had become a profession. . . ."

[7] Pp. 60, 61.

HEALTH

There are now fifty-four midwives in the township, all of whom attend the monthly meetings more or less regularly. The more active ones are brought in to work in the office with the nurse for a period of three months. The nurse reports that "all of the forty-five midwives have provided themselves with the regular midwife bag, properly lined with white washable material with pockets on both sides for holding each sanitary article," and twenty-eight have purchased the regular bags and equipment prescribed by the State Board. Thus under the nurse's careful instruction these superstitious practices have almost totally disappeared and it is very difficult to get the midwives to even discuss their former methods. This is undoubtedly the reason for the low infant death rate.

Much has been done but much remains to be done in the instruction of mothers in hygiene. Under the system of working out for wages, it is common for mothers to feed their babies at the breast in the morning and leave them under the care of one of the other children to be fed from a bottle during the rest of the day. In addition the poor nourishment of children under the care of old widows has been discussed. However, those children who attend Penn School are weighed and measured periodically and receive public health instruction so that, while a large proportion of these start in underweight and undernourished, their condition is greatly improved before the end of the first year. Thus both the fresh air, sunshine, and outdoor life on the Island and the efficient public health education render it a very healthy community.

CHAPTER VI

BREADWINNING

All the way,
All the way,
The Road is rough and rugged
All the way.

Sometimes I feel discouraged,
I don't know what to do.
The Road is rough and rugged
All the way.

Breadwinning on St. Helena Island pulses with nature's rhythms. The season, the tide, the storm, and the drought are forces far more pervasive and vital than the city dweller realizes. A good season brings bounteous crops. A good run of fish or shrimp supplements the larder and adds to the cash in hand. Spring tides which flood too high are disasters. "De dry drout" is a calamity. For many years soil and climate conspired to give the tidewater area a monopoly of sea island cotton. The boll weevil destroyed it in one season. The man attuned to nature still succeeds in securing a fairly decent living, but those whose habits do not harmonize barely eke out a precarious existence.

To understand the present economy it is necessary to remember that the boll weevil has changed the Sea Islands from communities in which farming predominated to communities in which it holds merely a secondary position. The majority shift from farming to fishing, work in the oyster canneries, or work on the public roads.

BREADWINNING

While this area had monopoly on long-staple silky sea island cotton everyone tended that crop. Life was relatively easy. With a little cultivation nature provided a fair yield of the staple which sold from one and a half to five times as much as the upland grades. The abounding fish, oysters, shrimp and crabs of the tidal creeks and the berries and nuts of the woods varied the family diet. Little more intensive cultivation brought a rich yield which was convertible into a sufficiency of ready cash. At ginning time the "yard" and the road leading to it were filled with lines of ox carts and wagons creaking with their loads of the snowy staple. The sea island cotton required a month longer to mature than the short staple and this extra month was all that the boll weevil needed to completely destroy the crop. It is for this reason that the few farmers who continue to raise cotton have switched to the less profitable short staple varities, and raise only a little of that. Since 1920, and the advent of the boll weevil, ginning time means nothing. For two years absolutely no cotton was harvested. Now a few farmers raise as much as a bale of short staple cotton. A few bring in cart loads or enough to sell for from $10 to $30, but the great majority raise none. This has meant discarding the old set of habits, abandoning the life that was built around sea island cotton. New objectives had to be found and new habits formed. The transition could not be made in eight years. The change is still in process.

Disregarding the few teachers, preachers and the island doctor, all of whom supplement their income by farming, there are now four rather distinct categories of breadwinners: First, a small group of about eighty-five farmers who put their major emphasis on the cultivation of the land. Even this group, however, derives almost as much of its income from outside wages as it does from cultivation of the land. This includes seven per cent of all the families. Second, is a large group of about six hundred, whose attention is divided between farming and wage-earning, and who derive between $50 and $100 in cash from their farms and enough produce to almost feed the family. Their outside earnings are slightly more than the proceeds from the cultivation of the soil. This includes 50 per cent of all families. Third, is a group of about four hundred and fifty who place their major dependence on the wages derived from work in the oyster canneries or near-by truck farms. This includes 37 per cent of all families. Fourth, is a group of about fifty old people who, in a city, would normally be dependent upon their relatives or upon charity, but who, owning land and house, are able to eke out an existence by gardening a little, by raising some poultry and pigs, picking up a dollar here and a dollar there at odd jobs, and receiving sporadic remittances from children in the city.

The successful farmer group includes people who have been able to adapt their habits to the new farming conditions. The middle group are those whose habits are partially adapted, and the wage-earning group are those who have given up farming as a bad job. These groups are not fixed. A few successive bad crop years would discourage a number who are now farming and drive them toward wage-earning or the abandonment of their treasured land for the city. On the other hand, the development of a really successful money crop to replace cotton would provide the necessary incentive to shift the emphasis now placed on wage-earning back to the cultivation of the land. This process of trial and error is now going forward. Farmers are looking for money crops to substitute for cotton. Others try farming for a while and then go back to wage-earning to recoup losses. Still others leave the Island entirely for a period and then come back to try out the vicissitudes of nature and agricultural economics.

The tragedy of this transition, the campaign for diversification conducted by Penn School in preparation for the boll weevil, the staunchness of the women standing by their husbands in the field, in developing poultry as a money crop of their own, and in putting up thousands of cans of vegetables and fruits for the pantry, is a romance of farm life worth tracing for its own interest as well as for the insight which it gives to the problems which are faced by farm communities throughout the nation.

The people of St. Helena can hardly be said to conduct their affairs in conformity with a money economy. So much of their goods and services is produced at home that an effort to express their standard of living in money results in an almost unbelievably small total. Those who are accustomed to such statistical expressions as "the average income in the United States is $3,347," [1] or the "average city laborer's family needs $1,500" to maintain a satisfactory standard of living, can hardly realize that a family can even subsist on less than $450 per year. The figures would suggest a poverty-stricken and drab life.

[1] National Bureau of Economic Research figures for 1926.

And yet this is what the average family on the Island not only subsists upon but manages to use to secure a reasonable degree of contentment. This is a yeoman economy which seeks its satisfactions not so much in terms of money as of unhurried and happy living.

Incomes on the Island are derived from such uniform sources in such simple ways that it was relatively easy to secure fairly accurate estimates of the budget. In the first place practically all income is clear. The most successful farmers buy a few sacks of fertilizer costing from $5 to $15 and seeds costing less than $5. A very few supplement their family labor by hiring extra help to the extent of $20 or $30 during a season and this is often paid for in produce. So that the highest gross incomes, with only $40 or $50 deducted, become net incomes and the great majority of gross incomes are clear. Inventory losses through sale and death of pigs, cattle and poultry over a period of years are usually balanced by gains through the breeding of young stock.

The average Island income for all groups [2] was $420 of which $275 was in money and $145 was in produce (including an allowance of $72 for use of the owned home). A few exceptional incomes ranged above $1,000 and the few old widows and widowers reported incomes of less than $100, but the large majority ranged from $250 to $600.

That this yeoman economy with its small amount of cash money is not peculiar to St. Helena Island or to the colored

---

[2] The income was secured by enumeration of 800 of the 1,200 Island families. The enumerators were checked by second visits to some families and the results found to be accurate for the purpose of calculating averages. These results are summarized in Table X, Appendix.

people is evidenced by some findings of the North Carolina State Tax Commission in its survey of farm incomes. When the returns from the white farmers in mountain counties came in, the Tax Commissioners were hardly prepared to believe that the farmers in this section subsisted on such a small amount. Yet a careful check revealed that the mountain farmers, with an average of 123 acres, had average cash receipts of $505. Of this $144 was derived from outside wages. As against this $505 our study shows $418 as the average cash receipts of the better St. Helena farmers,[3] whose holdings average only 15 acres. Outside wages made up $226 of their $418 cash income. The value of produce from the farm consumed by the mountain farm family was $439, while the family-living of better St. Helena farmers was about $190. The average income on St. Helena is about the same as that of the Negro farmers of Greene and Macon Counties, in Georgia, recently studied by Mr. Arthur Raper.

The most prosperous of the four groups on the Island is the one whose major emphasis is on farming. Their average income is $608, of which $418 is in cash. Their larger earnings are not so much attributable to superiority in farming as to their greater energy. The same enterprise which makes them successful in farming drives them at off times to tend store, to do carpentering, and in various other ways earn outside money. The average wage for the whole Island is only $212 and these successful families average $226 in wages. Thus, in addition to conducting the most successful farm operations, these men and their families are above the average in wage-earning capacity.

[3] Those included in Group I who devote their major time to farming.

But they never neglect the farm. They are always ready to drop other work when farm duties are pressing.

The group which mixes farming and wage-earning averages about $335 per year, of which about half is from wages and half from the farm. Both in agricultural production and wage-earning these are considerably below the more energetic group.

The group which depends largely upon wage-earning includes a few carpenters, drivers, porters and many laborers in the oyster canneries. The labor in oyster canneries, of which there are two on St. Helena and one on Ladies Island, is on the piece work basis, men receiving 15 to 25 cents per bushel for gathering the oysters and women 10 cents per can for shucking and putting them up. This group averages in total family income $480, of which $317 is in wages, and $163 in produce and use of the owned home.

These wage-earning opportunities have to an extent retarded agricultural rehabilitation. The oyster season runs from November through April and if the laborer is occupied for the whole period in the factories winter plowing and spring planting are often neglected. It is for this reason, in addition to the low scale of labor in the canning industry, that those interested in agriculture are apprehensive as to the devotion of much energy to wage-earning by the heads of island families.

On the other hand, during the serious depression caused by the boll weevil, ready cash has been hard to come by from farm operations. In this situation the wages offered by such seasonal labor have been a God-send to many families who required cash to pay taxes and to purchase the bare necessities of clothing, school tuition, church dues and such food as was not produced at home.

The phenomenon of "commuting" farmers, who earn their cash by labor away from home and partially support the family with produce from the land, is not confined to St. Helena, but has appeared, with the agricultural depression, in many places. In the piedmont cotton mill belt, numbers of farmers commute to the cotton mills for part time and, in certain districts in France, breadwinners share their energies between farming and day labor. It is a condition which probably will become more common as agriculture becomes relatively less profitable.

Other opportunities to earn money are utilized by a few who tend store or do carpentry. The principal merchandizing is done by one large firm with several branches on the Island. This is owned by white men. Soon after the Civil War several demobilized northern soldiers opened stores which, except in periods of unusual depression, have prospered. As long as cotton was almost exclusively grown, these concerns bought the farmers' produce as well as selling him his supplies. Competition and fairness kept prices within bounds. The great spread between cash and credit prices, usually found in the black belt, is not charged in the island stores.[4] Prices paid for cotton have also been fair. Since competition has ceased, during the past few years, there has been some complaint that the better grades of staple do not get their proper premium, but there is no evidence that the practices of the store in buying cotton are

[4] A recent study of farm credit in North Carolina revealed that Negroes pay 35 per cent for fertilizer credit and 28 per cent for merchant credit.

any more disadvantageous to the farmer than those of the average cotton buyer.[5]

There has, therefore, been no especial temptation to the colored people to enter merchandizing and they have lacked the capital to lay in a sufficient stock or extend sufficient credit to meet the Island's needs. There are, however, ten or twelve plantation stores or shops which buy from five hundred dollars' to seven hundred dollars' worth of goods wholesale from the main store and serve as convenient local buying points for staples. These are tended by Negroes, usually men who farm part time and tend store part time. That they are not lacking in shrewdness in their business deals is indicated by Uncle Sam Polite's explanation of the conditions of a loan imposed on a borrower who was a poor moral risk. "What I want," he said, "is a puyore mortgage on something that caint daid and ten cent on de dollar."

Midwifery is another means of earning outside money with fifty-three women. With so many in this profession, however (one to each three births), this cannot be very lucrative except to a few of the most popular.

It was remarked that from a money economy standpoint the average income of $420 would suggest a depressingly low standard of living. Writers on rural standards, however, are careful to point out that the farmer's standard of living is not comparable in money to that of the city dweller.

[5] Prof. R. H. Montgomery of the University of Texas in his *Cooperative Pattern in Marketing Cotton*, gives striking evidence of the inability of free competition to secure just prices for cotton, especially its failure to secure the proper premium for the finer grades.

BREADWINNING 123

In the first place the city laborer's entire income is in dollars which must, in turn, be spent for food, clothing, and rent at city prices. The farmer's calculated income includes an allowance of 6 per cent of the value of his house, for rent, which is often far less than he would have to pay for such a house in the city. It includes an allowance for food products raised at home and consumed by the family. This allowance is usually based on farm prices. A bushel of sweet potatoes is credited to the farmer's income at from $1 to $1.25 because that is the price for which he could sell it. But these potatoes would cost the city dweller almost twice as much.

There is also much self-service on the farm for which the city dwellers would pay. The average farmer has the time, and many have the inclination, especially when trained by such an institution as Penn School, to be general handy men. With hammer and saw they improve their own dwellings, and the housewife's needle makes the clothes last longer than the average city dweller's wardrobe. With their own crude millstones they convert their corn into meal and the wives convert the meal into bread. It is immaterial to them whether bakery prices are eight cents or ten cents a loaf. These services can hardly be estimated as income or expenditure but if they could they would materially increase the budget.

The details of how $420 are stretched to a competency for a family of four or five should prove instructive to the family which is mainly concerned with outspending its neighbors.

Judging from health and longevity the diet of the majority of the Islanders is ample. The annual average of $92 worth of home-grown produce consumed represents, for families in general, from ten to fifteen bushels of corn, a few chickens and eggs, several bushels of sweet and Irish potatoes, two or three bushels of field peas and garden truck, some of which is canned. A number of the more energetic farmers add to this list home-cured hog meat, from fifty to two hundred pounds, some sugar cane and cane syrup, peanuts, figs, benny [sesame], melons and turkeys. This diet, supplemented by purchases of flour, salt, sugar, side meat and canned goods secured from the store, is one not to be deprecated. It has often been commented by visitors to the Island that the large general store is remarkable as a country store for the good quality of the merchandize. This is true both of the food and clothing materials. Many of the Islanders insist on getting the best. Such unusual things as good brands of honey were found on the shelves. And the investigators in the field were pleased to be able to secure from the store a good brand of canned goods which had not been available in the university town which they left. Seemingly the teeming creeks are not resorted to for crabs, shrimp, oysters, and fish as much as they might be, though this potential supply is ever present as a variant from everyday fare.

The store divides the sales of clothing with mail order houses. Every mail brings in many packages from outside, but calicoes and denims are secured locally. It has been mentioned that the clothing lasts longer by reason of the fact that such a large number of women and men sew and cobble. Everyday wear is cotton and denim but each person has a good and neat (even if old) turnout for Sundays. The dress of the crowd at church or on a holiday

BREADWINNING 125

is sober but creditable to any rural community. There is considerable pride in neat appearance. When one of the investigators wished to photograph a group working in a cabbage field they objected seriously to being taken in their work clothes. "We won't have you take us nekkid," they explained.

While only $72 [6] is allowed as income for use of the average owned house, the dwellings are, for the most part, better than the houses usually furnished farm tenants of either race. Although it is difficult to compare such diverse dwellings, it is safe to say that the island dwellings averaging over three rooms with plenty of light and air are far superior houses to the one and two-room tenements occupied by so many migrants in the city who pay eight and ten dollars a week for these cramped quarters.

Lights go out early on the Island, often only the fire is used. Reading is done by kerosene lamps. The neighboring woods and thickets provide the fuel which, with the exception of a few days in the winter, is used only for cooking.

Church contributions are small but regular with practically all the families. The deacons stand in front of the congregation counting the money as the people sing a spiritual and march up and deposit their contribution on a table. As soon as the last one has come forward they announce "Thanks for the $17.41" or whatever the amount may be. Lodge dues and insurance hardly average fifty cents per month. Few books and practically no magazines are bought. Recreation is spontaneous rather than commercialized. The store manager tells of one picnic when

---

[6] An allowance of 6 per cent on a valuation of $1,200.

the cash register rang over six hundred times for sales which averaged about six cents apiece, showing that fun on the Island is not dependent on night-club prices. Such occasions are none the less fun.

On the whole this yeoman economy is not typically American in that it is not geared to money. The people show no inclination to strive to earn large sums only to pay them out again in large prices. The older generation seem to derive reasonable satisfaction from this standard. The younger have their eye on the glitter of the city. The chief objection to the present plane of living for the older generation is that it allows no surplus. Little was saved during the sea island cotton régime and much of that was wiped out in a recent bank failure with the result that few families have surplus to make necessary improvements or to provide a reserve against misfortune.

The attainment of this standard of living was not a natural result of landownership alone but is one of the results which a very real type of education has brought to the people. Penn School, with its genius for meeting the everyday problems of the community, has long devoted a large share of its program to raising the standards of the people. This has been especially true during the last twenty-five years.

In slavery the people were fed according to the plantation plan. The slaves, and the generation which immediately followed, lacked the chance to improve their diet. Miss Cooley, in her *Homes of the Freed*, relates that as late as twenty-five years ago, grits, white meat and sweet potatoes were the staples and green vegetables were considered fit only for the stock. Between the lines of her book the reader senses the long slow struggle of the Penn School workers to encourage year-around gardening and more wholesome preparation of the food with the result that at present kitchen stoves and adequate equipment have replaced the fire-place in many homes. And the women of the Island are particularly proud of their gardens and poultry.

In conservation of clothing, curtains, and bedclothes, the school has also moulded new ideas for the housekeepers. At first there was a struggle in Penn School to substitute buttons for pins, and to create for overalls and aprons an honored place as garments for everyday wear.

For a long time this work was carried on as a part of the school activity by the regular school teachers. The first definite community activity in this direction was the organization of the Community Class, a group of island house mothers who assembled regularly at the school to improve their homemaking. Miss Cooley relates her early failures with this group. First, in attempting to teach basketry, which was not popular because basket-making is considered a man's trade. When she sought to teach the Bible her efforts were coolly received because she was suspected of being a "Presbylocian" instead of a Baptist. But finally the interest of the women was fired by talks on home nursing and homemaking and the perfunctory meeting became "We Class." The women gathered at the school, singing spirituals, with nodding heads and swaying bodies, as they made quilts and other household articles and converted work into one of the regular social functions of the week. The school has always had intensively practical and thorough courses in cooking and sewing for the girls which center in a model home on the school grounds where all the phases of housekeeping are demonstrated and practiced.

For a number of years the school has conducted a sales house which disposes of second-hand garments sent down by friends of the Islanders. These are exchanged, sometimes for money, sometimes for produce, and in special cases of need they are given away. This has been a great help with the island wardrobes.

More recently the homemaking activities of the island women have had the specialized direction of a home demonstration agent who works from the school and is partially supported from the school budget. A typical schedule of her projects is as follows: garden campaign, beautification of grounds, poultry breeding and sales, okra acre sales, miscellaneous sales, food conservation and canning. She has ten women's clubs, and eight girls clubs, including about two hundred and fifty members.

Let us attend one of these club meetings with her: The meeting is called for 11 o'clock at a house which nestles in a flat expanse of fertile land, immediately back of the towering ruins of an old plantation house which has been gutted by fire, but whose enduring walls of oyster shells and sand tabby are a monument to the white civilization which died in 1865.

As is often the case with the colored people's meetings, the audience assembles slowly, although the four-room house of the hostess had been swept and garnished hours in advance and a bright fire prepared. Those who come early, however, fill in the time with neighborhood gossip

CANNING EXHIBIT

DOMESTIC SCIENCE

BREADWINNING 129

and spirituals. *Oh, Lead me to the Rock that is Higher than I, Thou hast been a Shelter for Me,* and *Heaven is a Beautiful Place, I know, I know. All Good Christians Over There, I know, I know,*" are feelingly and somewhat quaintly rendered.

Finally a neatly dressed matriarch of about seventy, the president of the club, is the last of the twelve members to arrive. Proceedings start with a prayer, "Lord, prop us up in grace and keep our weak knees from bending. Thou canst help us to bear the burden in the heat of the day."

A very formal "movement" is made for the hearing of the minutes of the preceding meeting. Then, with alacrity, the business of the morning is taken up. This is the selection of the canning outfit to be bought by the club and used cooperatively. There is a serious consideration of the problem as to whether to buy a $17.50 or $22.50 canner. It consists not so much of discussion as of wistful examination of the pictures in the catalog. Finally after the report that there is $14.25 in the treasury and that plans are underway for a rummage sale to raise the balance, it is decided to purchase the $22.50 outfit provided it would hold as many as two dozen cans.

The other item of business is swapping experiences on turkey raising. As the experiences go around the room, one woman could not wait for her turn, but popped up and related breathlessly how someone had given her three "tuckrey aigs the year before. De hawk leave me one of dese, and from that one I raise $48.50 worth tukries. No matter if I work out during the day on the buckras truck farm, I always come home and feed my tukries at noon."

But this was a meeting of a new club. The better established clubs have meal planning and demonstrations of muffins, biscuits, rolls, griddle cakes, cookies, and pies; and discussions of such topics as: How often should the beds be dusted, why should we dust our beds, how often should the mattress be turned, why is it necessary to turn our mattress, how many sheets should we use when making a bed, how should the second sheet be put on, how often should the bed and the bed covering be aired?

In the period of scanty rations precipitated by the boll weevil, the work of the canning clubs, supervised by the home demonstration agent, has filled an elementary need in feeding many families. From a small beginning a number of years ago, when a few women gathered at the school and brought their vegetables in in a cart to can them in the school canner, the idea of food conservation has spread over the Island until there are now nine clubs, each owning its own canner. In a year they put up over five thousand quarts of fruits and vegetables, four hundred quarts of jelly and preserves, and four hundred quarts of pickles and fruit juices. The example of these women is also followed by some who are not club members, but who can their produce on their own kitchen stoves at home.

It is learned from the report of the demonstration agent that women are encouraged to get their jars washed thoroughly and put on to sterilize before they begin to can their fruits and vegetables. They are also told that all things canned should be fresh and tender, and that a variety of things should be canned so that they can have fruits and vegetables regularly the year around.

The women's clubs also make household articles such as pillowcases, table-runners, table napkins, curtains, braided rugs, aprons and tablecloths. The demonstration agent is now focusing the interest of these clubs on pure-bred poultry and encouraging many of their members to cull their flocks so as to get better results from poultry-raising.

The girls' clubs, in addition to the interest in making simple articles of clothing and beautification of the home grounds, are encouraged to learn the culinary art by such contests as essays on food and garden projects, yeast bread contests and biscuit contests. There is considerable competition to be a judge in these toothsome contests and considerable interest and pride in the final reward.

It is through such simple but concentrated attention to the fundamentals that Penn School and its extension workers have been able materially to improve the wardrobe and diet. Perhaps in the long run the biscuit contest should appeal to the public mind as strongly as the beauty contest.

CHAPTER VII

AGRICULTURE

Keep yo' han' on de plow. Hold out.
Hold out. Hold out.
Keep yo' han' on de plow. Hold out.

Up on de mountain my Lord spoke.
Out of his mout' came fire and smoke.
Keep yo' han' on de plow. Hold out.

The chief method of breadwinning, agriculture, was well developed by 1920. The land was well tended and crops were balanced and rotated. Hard work was traditional. Nature gave special advantages for growing sea island cotton. The efforts of thoroughly trained farm demonstration agents and Penn School had developed an unusual vitality in the farming community. The advent of the boll weevil in 1920, however, removed sea island cotton, the keystone of the farm arch, with the result that the whole system went to pieces. It was an economic revolution which penetrated all phases of island life.

Here was a most cruel test of the stability of this Negro community. Their traditional means of livelihood was swept away overnight. The foundation of their agriculture collapsed. Against such fundamental economic forces the efforts of constructive workers would seem to be those of a David against a Goliath. It remains to be seen whether their ideas will prove to be the stone to overthrow the giant of depression, or whether the depressive forces

AGRICULTURE

will drive the farmers of this community to the city as they have driven thousands of other black belt farmers from communities where land ownership and educational activity were not present. This chapter indicates a valiant struggle to maintain community life, with the possibility that a general recovery in agriculture, following on the discovery of other money crops to supplement cotton, will once more restore the vigor of the community.

Agriculture in the Sea Islands traditionally depends upon the hoe and the ox rather than machinery, and upon compost rather than commercial fertilizer. It is further distinguished from farming in other parts of the black belt by the predominance of Negro landowners in contrast with tenants in other areas. The traditional ante-bellum culture of cotton determined the methods of tillage and the government's reconstruction policies fostered land ownership. The boll weevil and recent agricultural depression are forcing a new method of culture and endangering land ownership.

Reviewing briefly some of the history of the Island in its bearing upon agricultural conditions, it will be recalled that the lessons of farming were learned under the task system of slavery. Some of the field hands of those days are still active farmers and many of the present farmers are the sons of field hands taught at home. In the words of Uncle Sam, "De master been a good maan but de driber been a baad maan. He nebber lash me but once but he lash me sharp and he done me good. He learn me to wurk. Dese nyung nyankee chillun [1] dunno how to wurk."

[1] Uncle Sam refers to all children born in freedom as "nyankee chillun."

On the plantation the driver's horn blew at "day clean" [dawn]. Before that the women had to prepare breakfast and the hands repaired to the field. Varying numbers of tasks [quarter of an acre] were assigned and today the "task" survives as the unit of land estimation. The heavy work was largely done with hoes. Only a few of the more progressive farmers used plows. In winter some of the hands repaired to the marsh to cut grass, dig mud, and haul the mixture into compounds to rot as compost for the succeeding year's crop.

Little training was received by the field hands in the breeding and care of livestock. These were the duties of special stablemen and the field hands knew little of this important branch of farming.

Reconstruction brought possession of the land. In 1861 agents of the Treasury Department came to take up where the planters left off. The only change at first was that the Negroes were allowed wages for their work. Even before the agents came, however, and after the masters had left, the drivers were holding the hands together in the fields, partially through force of habit and partially because of the realization that the cultivation of the soil was their best chance to avoid starvation. For several years this persistence of the Negroes in working at their accustomed tasks even after their masters had left, fed them as well as produced thousands of bales of the valuable sea island cotton.

Some of the elements of independent farming had been introduced early. Most planters encouraged the raising of a certain portion of the food by allowing the slaves a food patch and poultry of their own. E. S. Philbrick, who

AGRICULTURE 135

operated a number of these plantations during reconstruction, speaks of his own cotton acres and the ex-slaves' food acres. This division was made presumably because he wished each family to cultivate its own food and work for wages upon the cotton crop.

The period enabled numbers of Negroes to save from their wages the fifteen dollars necessary to buy a ten-acre plot when the Federal Government subdivided [2] the plantations and sold the land to heads of families at the ridiculously low price of $1.50 per acre.

The long fields formerly cultivated as a unit were merely subdivided by surveyed lines. Ditches and hedges still mark their original boundaries. Houses formerly in "de street" or quarters were moved to the new home sites and animals purchased at the auctions of plantation effects or from the foragers of Sherman's Army.[3] The implements of the plantation and household furnishings were also auctioned off and the new system was well under way by 1868.

But when the freedmen were left alone with their lands, fortune did not always smile. While they knew how to work they had little experience in independently managing their affairs. Much of the choicest cotton seed had been shipped North with the cotton and planting had to proceed with inferior seed. The result was some disastrous crop failures in the beginning. They soon, however, became reasonably successful, small cotton farmers.

During the thirty-five year period after the withdrawal of the Government (from 1870 to 1904), they had little

[2] For the details of this subdivision see Chapter II.
[3] Philbrick, in *Port Royal Letters*, expresses apprehension at the high price and poor quality of animals thus purchased.

besides their own efforts to depend upon for progress. During this time Penn School, the only outside agency in the community, was a rather narrow, classical school, emphasizing the book subjects and giving little attention to community of problems. It was not until 1904, that the adoption of agricultural programs and community ideals brought to these farmers the aid of outside paternalistic philanthropy.

The ownership of the soil has been a determining factor in the lives of the St. Helena people. It has anchored them to the Island more effectively than tenancy could possibly have done and it has left the owners considerably more freedom to diversify crops than tenants are usually allowed.

In general, families value their holdings far above the money price which the lands will bring. They may scatter to different cities or cease cultivation of the major part of their tract but they usually scrape up tax money to hold their land. Often they return for short periods of residence and always, if possible, they wish to be buried in the plantation burying grounds. Almost every month sees several of them brought back on their last journey from Savannah or Charleston or even New York or Philadelphia to their final rest beneath the moss-grown oaks.

This tendency to hold on to the land for sentimental reasons even when it is not in use, together with the fact that there is little outside demand for farms on St. Helena, has run the price down to where the few tracts which do change hands are sold for only $5 or $10 an acre. So much good land is idle that it can be rented by anyone

AGRICULTURE

who will keep up the taxes, so that rent and taxes are about equivalent.

Another peculiarity of the landholdings on the Island is the extent to which they are involved in estates. The original purchasers have died and the present users are their grandchildren and sometimes their great-grandchildren. No one ever thinks of making a will and inheritance is therefore equal. Some original ten-acre tracts have been subdivided into two- and four-acre plots but most of these estates are held as units and operated by one or two of the heirs. One of the investigators bought a small plot of land on the Island and the deed had to be signed by eighteen grandchildren and great-grandchildren of the original purchaser. One man was found operating twenty-one acres. Six he had bought, five had been inherited by his wife, five from his uncle's estate, and five from the estate of one of her relatives.

Often the only way to definitely clear such confused titles is to allow the land to be sold for taxes and bid it in at sheriff's sale. Obviously the user of land whose ownership is scattered so widely has no great incentive to spend money to improve it. On account of the uncertainty of the title he cannot borrow money on mortgage for improvements. For this reason many of these little estates are not worked at all but simply lie idle.

On the other hand when the land is subdivided among so many heirs the tracts become so small that cultivation is not profitable. The island lands in this respect have approached the *morcellement* of the lands of the French peasant who owns several scattered small tracts.

For the type of farming done on the Island from two

to five acres are entirely too little to support a family. Nevertheless the enumeration of 1928 showed seventy-five farms of less than three acres (6 per cent of the total), and 404 or 31 per cent of the total were between three and ten acres. Only the exceptional farmers on the Island succeeded with less than ten acres (Table XI).

While this process of subdivision has proceeded rapidly there has been no reconcentration by men who add to their holdings through purchase. The island ambitions seem to be fixed on the twenty- to twenty-five-acre plot cultivated entirely by the family with little hired help.

The size of the farm operated varies from time to time. So many vacant holdings are near by that in prosperous times the energetic farmers can easily find additional tracts for cultivation. They can retrench by merely dropping some of these tracts out of cultivation. The really significant decrease is in the number of farms over twenty acres. There were 366 of these in 1920, and five years of the ravages of the boll weevil decreased them to 202. The 1928 enumeration showed 266 tracts of over twenty acres in operation, but many of these were only partially cultivated. This indicates a recovery in farming since the first severe shock administered by the boll weevil. This recovery is also apparent in the figures as to livestock owned which are quoted later.

This severe curtailment in acreage during the first five years of the boll weevil is indicated by the sharp drop in acreage cultivated from 1920 to 1925. (See Table XII.) During these five years all land in farms decreased 3,300 acres or 13 per cent. Crop land harvested decreased 8,000 acres or 54 per cent. The sweet potato acreage

AGRICULTURE 139

was cut by 3,000, the corn acreage by 2,500, and the cotton acreage 1,800. It is evident that the demoralization of cotton planting was accompanied by severe reduction in other branches of farming also. Other crops were incidental to cotton culture and when it was abandoned, the people left their farms for work elsewhere. The ridge pole having collapsed, the rafters caved in.

The land is tilled with primitive plows drawn by oxen or small island ponies. The two-horse plow is never used. The sandy black loam is turned in the winter, and in early spring the rows are listed. A compost mixture of rotted marsh grass, mud, and barnyard manure is spread in the rows. This method of fertilizing has come down from slavery days. For sea island cotton, it was a rather efficient method; but judging from yields of other crops now produced, it is not nearly so effective as commercial fertilizer. The gathering of this marsh mud and cutting of marsh grass is a heavy winter task. From two hundred and fifty to five hundred cartloads are used on the more successful farms. Men and boys and sometimes women go out in bateaux on the tidal creeks, and plunge bare-legged into the marsh with sickle and shovel to fill their boats with grass and mud. Next they haul this "maash" to the barnyards, where it is rotted during the winter and mixed with manure. This is back-breaking work and necessitates long hours out on the water and marsh.

Later cultivation of the crop is done with the turn plow and in a few instances with the sweep or walking cultivator, and in many cases with the heavy island hoes wielded by several members of the family. Thus the equipment of the average family is an ox and a pony or two, a plow, a harrow and sometimes a sweep and cart, all of which could be bought for a few dollars. However, by the middle of the season, unless too much rain has intervened the crops seem clean and well tended.

Corn has always been the crop occupying the major acreage. There were five acres in corn to three in cotton in 1920. Though the Islanders plant almost twice as many acres to corn as they plant to cotton, the general average among Negro farmers of South Carolina is just the reverse since they plant practically twice as many acres to cotton as they do to corn. This is a good index of the greater diversification on island farms.

Corn is necessary for the family, the animals, and the poultry. Usually from three to six acres are planted. The yield is not so large as could be obtained by better cultivation and fertilization. The usual yield is around 15 bushels to the acre [4] and the better farmers make from 25 to 30 with an occasional yield of about 50 bushels, while some of the white farmers and colored farmers, especially supervised by the demonstration agent, get 50 and 60 from soil which has been better tended and fertilized.

Cotton is still raised by a few farmers and, with sweet potatoes and peanuts and poultry, it supplies the cash income from the farm. However, the cotton raised is the short-staple variety and not the long-staple sea island which was once the island farmer's specialty and chief dependence.

About the only other change in culture has been the shift

---

[4] The general average corn yield for South Carolina is 12 bushels per acre.

of cotton fields from the lower, wetter lands to the higher ridges. The low, and even brackish, lands formerly produced the best sea island cotton, but it is impossible to use them for short staple cotton when the boll weevil is present. The acreage in cotton per farm has also been materially reduced, a condition which is vital to the successful handling of the weevil. In 1919, 900 farms reported 3.6 acres per farm in cotton. In 1924, 825 farms reported 1.8 acres per farm. Thus the cotton acreage was more than cut in two.

In respect to other measures for combating the weevil, the adaptation to the new habits necessary to grow cotton successfully has not been made. Hard work is relied upon rather than fertilizer or poisoning. In the season of 1929 only twenty-five tons of fertilizer were sold to all the island farmers by the store and forty-eight by the Cooperative Society and this was purchased by a small minority of the total number. The great mass still depends entirely upon compost.

Only two farmers were found who used a really adequate amount of fertilizer.[5] The others fertilize only a part of their acreage or spread an inadequate amount over too much land. As long as this system is followed cotton yields will be low. The emphatic recommendations of agricultural experts are that high grade fertilizers, heavily applied, be used as the best means of bringing the crop in ahead of the heavy boll weevil damage.

The more direct means of combating the weevil, i.e., picking up and burning infested squares and applying the

---

[5] Fertilization to the extent of 1,200 pounds per acre is recommended by the farm demonstration agent for cotton.

poison, are resorted to only in a dilatory fashion. The idea that the weevil is a divine dispensation and should not be disturbed is still quite prevalent. One old fellow when asked about what measures he used to combat this pest, said, "What, me fight dat bug? De Lord sent him here and I can't do nothing about it."

The habit of planting cotton leads many to cling on to the crop, and the fatalistic attitude toward the weevil and the lack of fertilizer has cut the average yield to less than a quarter of a bale to the acre. It is a real puzzle to the island farmers as to whether or not they should plant cotton and each spring there is much head-scratching as to how many acres to devote to the crop. The uncertainty of the winter temperature and moisture conditions contribute to wide fluctuations in the yield under weevil conditions.

The other principal money crops are sweet potatoes, peanuts, and occasionally Irish potatoes. The latter are not raised extensively because of the capital necessary for fertilizer and the fluctuation of the farm price. After the boll weevil came, considerable attention was devoted to the Irish potato crop and the yield between 1919 and 1924 was doubled on about the same number of acres. However, a number of the farmers went into this crop heavily in 1928 and there was a marked over-production all through the Eastern Coast, reducing the price to a point where it hardly paid to dig potatoes. Sweet potatoes yield on the average of about twenty bushels to the acre with much higher yields when well cultivated and fertilized. They are a fairly steady source of money income as they can be marketed regularly. Peanuts also yield very well

AGRICULTURE

in the soil of the Island, but only about one-half acre per farm is usually planted. It is, therefore, necessary for the Cooperative Society to assemble the product of its members into marketable lots. Undoubtedly one of the most hopeful possibilities in island farming is in the direction of wider utilization of these peanut and potato crops.

In recent years the oyster canning plants have experimented with the canning of tomatoes and okra in the summer and these crops are coming into favor with a few of the farmers. Some of them did very well with their tomatoes in 1928. One man raised 14,000 pounds on an acre or about $85 worth.

The miscellaneous food crops include a little rice raised in the wet spots, cow peas grown by over two-thirds of the farmers, and soy beans, sugar cane, and melons.

It would be well before leaving this discussion to emphasize the difference between this type of farming and that done by the Negro farmer of the black belt, especially that of the Negro tenants, who, before the advent of the boll weevil, were held strictly to cotton and knew very little about raising food crops and animals. The farmers on St. Helena have been more self-sufficient, planting more land to corn than cotton and about as much land to sweet potatoes as to cotton and adding to these a miscellany of other crops to balance their income and diet.

The relative self-sufficiency of the island farmers as contrasted with the black belt tenants is as evident in the possession of animals as in the diversification of crops. Practically every farm has a cow and calf and either an ox or a horse. Until recently some of the farms had both animals, and a few had two horses or oxen.[6] Each farm also had several pigs and a flock of poultry.

For the first few years after the boll weevil, there was a tendency to sell off some of these animals to raise cash. The number of horses was reduced about 160[7] and the number of cattle about 300, the number of pigs fell from 4.4 per farm in 1920 to 1.3 in 1925. Thus the farm capital was heavily drawn upon to struggle through "de haad times." From 1925 to 1928, however, the indications are that these losses of animals are being replaced, especially in the pigs, where 70 per cent of the farmers now report 1.7 per farm.

The flocks of chickens were greatly reduced during the hard times. From 1920 to 1925 the average drop was from twenty-four to ten per farm, but in the last three years this average rose again to twelve per farm and in the meantime there has been considerable increase in the breeding of turkeys. In 1928 half of the farmers were raising turkeys with about two breeding hens per farm. Poultry has become a source of considerable income and a number of families look upon revenues from this source as certain to provide the necessary tax money. This is especially true of the island turkeys which seem to thrive on their natural diet which they are able to pick up in the field. Better methods of standardizing, fattening, and marketing (which could be stimulated by the Cooperative Society) would greatly increase the revenue from this source since most of the flocks are not culled and are poorly housed. It has been the experience of those who purchase the St.

[6] The work animals used by the black belt share tenant are usually the property of the landlord and are used by the tenant only for farm duties.

[7] Some of this loss in horses was owing to a severe epidemic.

AGRICULTURE

Helena turkeys that from two to six pounds can be added to their weight with great improvement in flavor when they are penned closely and carefully fed for five or six weeks.

There is also much room for improvement in the care and breeding of livestock. The animals are not only small in size, but very poorly fleshed. The island stock is naturally small and the animals also lack proper and sufficient feed. Except on the better farms they are poorly fed, and poorly cared for, the outbuildings being in many cases open-sided sheds.

Primitive methods are also followed in pasturage. Only one or two fenced pastures were found on the Island. The usual custom is to tie the animal by a long rope secured to a peg and allow it to graze in a circle. This method is even followed with pigs so it is not at all unusual to see perfect circles where they have uprooted the ground to feed.

Fenced pastures would undoubtedly be of a benefit to the livestock, but with such small holdings, individual fenced pastures are impractical because they would neither leave enough land for cultivation nor contain sufficient land to furnish pasturage. However, with the amount of vacant land on the Island there is nothing except the individualism of the farmer which stands in the way of co-operative leasing and fencing of these tracts or the employment of a common herdsman and developing them into excellent common pastures. It would seem that the grazing method wears out enough rope to pay for quite a bit of fence wire. Such pastures, together with a few well bred stallions, bulls and boars, would undoubtedly be valuable additions to the Island's economy.

The summary of the fore-going discussion reveals that there are several serious handicaps to farming, in addition to the disastrous effects of the boll weevil. These are: (1) The subdivision of a large proportion of the tracts, by equal inheritance, into plots entirely too small for profitable farming. (2) The entailment of many other tracts in undivided estates, where the rights of the operator of the farm are shared with a number of other heirs. (3) Periodical storms or hurricanes which occasion losses of the total crop. (4) Marketing difficulties which, up to the time of the building of the bridge, practically prohibited the selling of anything but staple crops. (5) The failure to save any considerable amount of money from the cash received from sea island cotton and the loss of the greater proportion of money saved in a recent bank failure. All these, in alliance with the boll weevil, have been arrayed against the natural advantage of soil and climate, the traditional love of the land, and the educational forces of the school and the farm demonstration agent.

From this welter of conflicting forces one group of fairly successful farmers stands out. It has been noted that some eighty-five men who constitute 7 per cent of the heads of families are making a success of farming in spite of the difficulties. Why these should succeed where the others merely drift or fail is a question of deepest significance, not only to the future of the Island, but also to the more general efforts to rehabilitate agriculture. For it is possible in practically all other farming communities to find a parallel of this successful group of men who have in a measure succeeded in spite of agricultural depression.

AGRICULTURE

Here we have the clear illustration of Seligman's [8] contention that in agriculture the marginal man tends to hold on longer than in other occupations. In business or industry the marginal man, the near-failure, is soon forced out through inability to earn a livelihood. But a farmer who possesses his land can at least grow enough food to keep the wolf from the door, even though his farming operations may be relatively inefficient.

It was noted in the previous chapter that there are some six hundred heads of families who divide their time between agriculture and day labor on the outside. These are the marginal farmers whose operations are, for the most part, relatively unproductive; while the eighty-five men in the successful group are somewhat above the margin, rather close to it since the coming of the boll weevil, but nevertheless far enough above to earn a fairly good living for their families. This condition raises a serious question as to whether or not one of the causes of the present general depressed condition in agriculture is the effort of too large a proportion of the people to continue farming. It focuses attention on the kind of people who are endeavoring to farm, as well as upon the situation in which they are farming.

These successful farmers were studied more closely than the other breadwinners in an effort to learn just what were the traits which make them successful where others fail. The question was raised as to whether these men had farmed all their lives while others had divided their attention. This was not a complete explanation of success, because while we find John Henderson on one hand who

[8] Seligman, E. R. A., *The Economics of Farm Relief*.

has always been relatively successful since his apprenticeship on his father's farm, we find Ben Chaplin, on the other hand, who up until five years ago was practically down and out. He had tried various kinds of wage-earning jobs and storekeeping with little success. His latter adventure had involved him deeply in debt. However, several years ago, he appeared at the door of one of his creditors with a bale of cotton to begin paying up. Under the influence of the demonstration agent, he had determined to go back to farming and put all of his energy into an effort to succeed with the land. The result was that within three years he was not only out of debt, but actually extending his operations by renting additional land. One year he raised a fraction over five bales of cotton on five acres and in 1928 he had an income of about one thousand dollars from his farm, and some additional cash from a small store. Another possible factor of success which was investigated was the size of landholding but this was also not a complete differentiation. None of the really successful men had very small tracts, and only one or two had less than ten acres. Their general average holding was only fifteen acres. But there are several hundred other farmers on the Island who hold this much land but do not cultivate it successfully. So the mere possession of an adequate acreage is not sufficient to bring success.

Intelligence in planning the use of land was a factor of some note. It was found, for instance, that practically all of these successful farmers planted enough corn (from three to six acres) to yield a supply for their families and animals. Most of the unsuccessful farmers on the other hand had to resort to the purchase of corn before the succeeding crop came in.

Another factor of significance was that practically all of these successful men had married energetic wives. In fact, for a long time, one of these couples divided their land and competed with each other in their farm operations. The woman's part, in addition to the housekeeping duties, included the care of the poultry, some of the care of the animals and a share in the actual field work. Several of the successful farmer group proved to be widows who were carrying on the work in the absence of the male head of the family. But this factor likewise fails to account for the success, for the successful farmers cannot be supposed to have a monopoly on the hard-working women.

In short, there is no wide distinction between the successful and unsuccessful in the system followed. All of the personal factors of success were found to be present to some extent in the unsuccessful group. It would, therefore, seem that the key to success lies in the favorable combination of several of these factors,—sound habits of farming, the possession of enough land, intelligence in planting and tillage, and energy.

This leads us to the feeling that there are intangible differences in personality which lead these men to do the right thing at the right time and not to dilly-dally or delay. In a sense it may be said that their personalities are more adapted to cooperation with the soil and nature.

It is somewhat discouraging to note from the ages of these successful farmers that many of them will soon pass out of the picture without a proportionate number of younger members of the group to replace them. Of the eighty-four, only thirteen are below forty and fifty-three are above fifty.

In the effort to meet the discouraging agricultural depression the whole range of farm life has been concentrated upon by Penn School with its farm and home demonstration agents. The result is that a larger proportion of the farmers are making a living in this than in other Negro agricultural communities and that the population has held on to their lands better.[9] The completeness of this constructive program is worthy of detailed description.

The agricultural activities of the school extend back twenty-five years to the time when the realities of education as practised by Hampton Institute were transferred to Penn through the interest of Dr. Hollis P. Frissell upon the Board of Trustees and co-principalship of Misses Cooley and House, who were formerly Hampton teachers.

These ladies began agricultural demonstration lessons with what Miss Cooley describes as a blind horse, a leaky old barn and old worn-out cotton land which would produce only from seven to twelve bushels of corn per acre. Gradually the agricultural activities have progressed as the visions of the principals expanded, as funds increased, as trained workers became available and as the interest of the people was aroused. The school now furnishes both

[9] Liberty County, Georgia, which contains a similar colony of Negro landowners living under very similar conditions, shows only a handful of Negro farmers who compare with the successful St. Helena group and the loss of population has been more heavy. Only one farmer in this section was really making a good living.

AGRICULTURE

instruction in farming and leadership for the community in all phases of agriculture. It leads because it has gained the confidence of the majority of the island leaders whether teachers, preachers, or professional farmers, and because it has spread the messages of diversification, good tillage, and energy applied to the soil. As far as it is possible for an institution to move a mass of human beings with their own traditions, habits and personalities, Penn School has reshaped agricultural policies.

The agricultural activities of the school are now carried on under the general supervision of the principals and with the general interest of all teachers. Three full-time people specialize in this field, the school farmer, the home demonstration agent and the farm demonstration agent. Agricultural instruction is given both at the school farm and on "home acres" assigned to the children by parents and cultivated under the direction of the school. The adults are reached through demonstration work, clubs, and exhibits. Even the graduating exercises of the school include a predominance of agricultural interests instead of stereotyped orations. The crowd is as interested and appreciative of a talk by one of the boys on the good points of a well-bred cow, as illustrated by the cow in person, as it would be in a debate.

The school has also fostered the organization of a Cooperative Association and a Credit Union. This was the first cooperative for either race to be organized in the state. These two organizations represent a set of ideas entirely foreign to the island farmers, who as a group were formerly dependent upon the general store both for credit and for purchase of their crops. They are gradually taking hold of these phases of agricultural economics but are greatly in need of constructive leadership.

The Cooperative Society is the older of the two and includes some forty-four members. About half of the successful farmers are in the Association and half have not yet learned the benefits of cooperation or acquired the willingness to cooperate.

So far the benefits of the Association have been derived more largely from cooperative buying than from cooperative selling of products. During the year 1928, 48 tons of fertilizers were purchased, 256 sacks of seed potatoes, 15 bushels of cotton seed and 1,500 barrels for shipping potatoes. In lots of this size, the cooperative was able to get a better price for its members than they could have gotten individually. The alliance of this Association with the Credit Union enables the farmer to secure these supplies as a loan where such assistance is needed.

During the same year four cars of sweet potatoes, three tons of peanuts and a few chickens were marketed cooperatively. The peanuts were sold for $90 a ton by holding them off the market until the price was favorable. They would have had to be sold for $76 a ton if they had been marketed when harvested.

With farms as small as those on the Island, the total amount of a crop produced is often too small to handle conveniently. A useful function of this Cooperative Association is assembling these odd lots into marketable quantities. As has been indicated, the cooperative can be of great value to the island farmer in advocating better methods of breeding and standardization of products. How-

AGRICULTURE

ever, if the organization is to extend into a larger field and make the necessary advances to the farmers while their products are being held for better prices, more capital will be needed for the Credit Union.

The Credit Union is an outgrowth of the cooperative for loaning money to its members for operating expenses. Its assets consist mainly of a $4,500 loan from the school. This money is loaned to the farmers at the rate of 7 per cent. The Credit Union really needs additional capital in order to go into the broader fields of standardization, and the proper fertilization of crops, and the proper housing and breeding of poultry. It is comparatively easy in a bad crop year to freeze assets of only $4,500 in loans which cannot be paid off until the succeeding year. The situation of the island farmers is acute, and the importance of this all-Negro community so strategic that easy loans, even to the extent of paternalism, would seem justified in an effort to bring the community through this agricultural crisis.

The persons through whom the agricultural activity of the school is carried to the adults of the community are the farm demonstration agent and the home demonstration agent. The work of the latter with the homes of the Island has been fully discussed in the preceding chapter.

Some idea of the range of the work of the farm demonstration agent is gained from the following organizations through which he works: Cooperative Association, Credit Union, Farmers' Fair Committee, Truckers' Club, Poultry Club, Tomato Club, Junior County Club, The Rosenwald School Committee. A description of the activities of two of these clubs will typify the character of their work.[10]

The Truckers Club was organized about four years ago. At its birth, it was known as the potato club and organized with six men to sell white potatoes cooperatively. So successful has been the work of this group in the sale of their potatoes that others made application for membership. It soon reached a total of sixteen members and instead of selling potatoes alone, it raised for market such crops as garden peas, tomatoes, cucumbers, and potatoes. The name was changed to the Truckers' Club and instead of depending on the one crop, a variety was grown. The club now has twenty-three members who are growing a better grade of truck crops and are handling them more intelligently on the market.

The Tomato Club was organized with seven members. A contract was entered into with one of the local canneries and these men agreed to grow the tomatoes to be canned. There was not a single failure and John Henderson made a yield of 14,019 pounds on one acre. So telling has been the result of this demonstration that the same cannery has entered into contract with sixty men for the growing of tomatoes and a man is being paid to follow up this particular line of work which the agent started.

In addition to this club work strategic farmers are persuaded to demonstrate a particular crop or a particular method of fertilization or tillage with the hope that the surrounding farmers will be aided by the example of these demonstrations. The schedule for demonstration in a typical year is as follows: 3 in cotton, 3 in corn, 5 in pea-

[10] From 1928 Report of Farm Demonstration Agent.

nuts, 15 in Irish potatoes, 6 in sweet potatoes, 4 in pruning and spraying fruit trees, 12 in horticulture, 9 in poultry, 6 in hogs, 3 in keeping farm accounts, 14 in soil improvement. Some typical results of these demonstrations are as follows: [11]

There were twelve result corn demonstrations started and carried through the year. Forty acres were involved in these demonstrations, the increased yield being twenty-two bushels. Twenty farms are planting improved seed as a direct result, ten farms are practicing seed selection, and ten farms are adopting a better cropping system.

Robert Heyward made the most outstanding yield of corn this year, raising fifty-three bushels to the acre on land sown in cow peas the previous season on which he used forty loads of manure and four hundred pounds of 8-3-3 fertilizer.

Peanut demonstrations were conducted to prove the worth of this crop to supplement cotton for cash and to furnish family food and animal feed. This section seems to be particularly adapted to the growing of this crop and yields of from eight hundred pounds to nine hundred pounds have been made under ordinary conditions. Eight method demonstrations were given in connection with the growing of peanuts, and five adult result demonstrations started and carried through the year. It was found that peanuts planted around April 15 in rows of thirty inches apart and twelve inches apart in the drill with an average of from four hundred to six hundred pounds of 8-4-4 fertilizer gave the best result. Crushed oyster shell is

[11] From 1928 Report of Farm Demonstration Agent.

often used to supplement the commercial fertilizer. William Cuthbert made a yield of 1,670 pounds of Spanish peanuts on one acre and if it were not for the storm, his yield would have easily been one ton to the acre, besides nearly two tons of a good grade of peanut hay. So impressed has been the district agent of Florence with this yield that he suggested that they go into peanuts more fully another year. With his aid, and the aid of our district agent, more demonstrations along this particular line will be conducted the coming year.

Ten new farms have been induced to plant improved seed, four farms are practicing seed selection, and two farms are adopting better methods in cropping and fertilizing this crop.

Thus the farm demonstration agent continually moves about in the community making practical suggestions as to improvement and methods and conducting demonstrations in better farming. The value of his work to the individuals touched can hardly be overestimated. The difficulty lies, however, in the fact that one man, however energetic he may be, can only reach a small proportion of the farmers of the community, and only a few people are able or willing to imitate the good results of the demonstrations set for them. Such activity is, therefore, but leaven in the lump, working with sureness but with tragic slowness against the rising tide of adverse economic conditions which beset the St. Helena farmer.

On the whole the results of constructive work with farmers have palliated rather than relieved the acute agricultural crisis. Always these landowners have grown a larger proportion of their food and have raised more domestic animals than tenant farmers. They were further prepared for the disaster to the cotton crop by more intensive effort toward food and feed culture. But the habits of cotton culture were well fixed and many lost their small surplus in the endeavor to continue cotton planting. On the other hand an encouraging number are making a living under the new system.

The movement cityward is of sufficient volume to deplete the community if continued for a long period without compensating influx from other communities. Here again St. Helena shares the tendencies of other areas in the cotton belt. The Island, however, is of strategic importance as a demonstration of what a Negro landowning community can become. For this reason especial efforts at colonization would be warranted. Colonization would be a semi-paternalistic interference with the normal economic and social forces, but if such interference could guarantee the continuance of the experiment on St. Helena it would be well worthwhile. With schemes of agricultural colonization being widely considered, St. Helena is worthy of consideration as the location of a colony. One of the stumbling blocks which has often caused agricultural colonies to fail has been the initial payment of too high a price for the land. Here, good fertile land can be obtained at from $5 to $10 per acre. At this price it should be possible to find Negro farmers who are ambitious to buy land, in sufficient numbers to repopulate the farms now vacant. This would guarantee the continuance of the community of Negro landowners in a place where the educational and social institutions are already developed to a high level.

CHAPTER VIII

TAXATION AND GOVERNMENT BENEFITS

Bear yo' burden,
Bear yo' burden,
Bear yo' burden in de heat ob de day.

An Islander does not discuss financial affairs for long before he complains about taxation. "De tak" on his small acreage, his goods and his "critters" seems to enter into many of his financial calculations.

The fact that the Islanders complain frequently and with feeling about the weight of their taxes scarcely distinguishes them from residents of other agricultural communities in all parts of the country. One of the major consequences of the general agricultural depression has been a widespread revolt on the part of farmers against what they conceive to be an unjust and crippling burden of taxation.

South Carolina, like other states, is endeavoring to lighten the burden of rural taxation by the apportionment of grants-in-aid, and by allowing local governments to share in the proceeds of certain state revenues. No part of the benefits of this state largesse inures to the township of St. Helena. The people, however, are not troubled by this omission. Even if they knew what state aid was, it is unlikely that they would expect to share in its benefits.

They undoubtedly feel that they have a tax grievance,

TILLING

POUNDING RICE

GOVERNMENT BENEFITS 159

but this grievance is not founded on the theory that the more wealthy communities of the state ought to contribute toward the maintenance of their roads and schools. Were they politically articulate, which they are not, they would draw up an exceedingly modest set of demands. Far from asking financial assistance from the more opulent sections of their county and state, they would ask merely that this formula be not reversed in their case. They would ask that the taxes collected on the Island be expended for purposes which benefit the Island, and that they no longer be required to contribute, out of their meagre incomes, toward the support of governmental activities which benefit sections of the country far wealthier than their own.

St. Helena Island, the territory comprised in the school district of St. Helena, has had an average annual tax bill of approximately $16,500 during the past seven years. (Table XIII.) About 78 per cent of this sum has gone to the county, 15 per cent to the state and the remaining seven per cent has represented township and district levies. The district has contributed over $6,000 per annum for roads and bridges, and $4,400 for schools. Levies for highways and schools account for about five-eighths of the total taxes collected.

Practically all these revenues are raised through two forms of taxation, the general property tax and the poll or capitation tax. Over 80 per cent of the total collections are attributable to the general property tax. (Table XIV.) Except for the increase in 1927 there has been little fluctuation in the tax rate during the past seven years. The average rate has been 3.8 per cent of the assessed valuation. In addition to the general property tax, all able-bodied males between the ages of twenty-one and sixty are subject to a poll tax of one dollar per annum, for the support of public education. There is also a commutation road tax of $3.50 per capita. This latter tax is in lieu of the time-honored provision which required all adult males to contribute a specified number of days' labor on highway maintenance work.

The tax payments of the Islanders are relatively higher because of their ignorance of the proper procedure in returning taxes and because of the inconveniences involved in making the returns. The assessing official visits the Island several times during the assessment period, but only comes for one day at a time to the central store, which is eight miles from some portions of the township. Under these conditions, and because of ignorance of the importance of tax returns, very many of the Islanders do not turn in their property and thereby incur the 50 per cent penalty on personal property which is assessed for failure to render the returns. In these cases the return for the former year is carried forward, and this gives rise to the continued assessment for animals which have died or been sold, and for various other chattels which have been lost or destroyed.

The $16,500 collected annually amounts on a per capita basis to $3.77 per inhabitant. As per capita tax payments go, this is an exceedingly modest sum. The per capita tax bill for the remainder of Beaufort County is $10.58, which is almost three times as high as the St. Helena figure. The comparative smallness of the amount which the average St. Helenite contributes toward the cost of government is even more apparent when it is considered

GOVERNMENT BENEFITS   161

that South Carolina, as a whole, has an average state and local tax bill of $21.39 per capita, and that the comparable figure for the United States as a whole is $48.69 per capita.[1]

It would be a mistake to conclude from the above comparisons, however, that the taxes paid on St. Helena do not constitute a heavy burden. It is axiomatic that the burdensomeness of a tax cannot be measured by its absolute amount. The heavy tax payments of the wealthy may involve no greater inconvenience than a slight curtailment of expenditure for luxuries. The few dollars exacted from the poverty-stricken individual who is barely managing to make ends meet may easily mean the denial of necessities. It is only when the tax payments of the inhabitants of St. Helena are related to their economic resources that the real burdensomeness of these payments is seen.

The ratio of taxes to income on St. Helena is about 4 per cent, whereas the corresponding ratios for the state as a whole and the United States are 4.9 and 5.6 respectively. (As shown by Table XV.) Taken by themselves these ratios do not indicate an excessive burden for St. Helena. The question of burdensomeness, however, assumes an entirely different aspect when attention is directed to the extremely low income level which prevails on the Island. The average income per family in the United States, as a whole, is $3,347. The per family income of South Carolina is $2,119.[2] Both of these incomes are large enough to permit the payment of a 5 or 6 per cent tax without trenching on fundamental necessities. On the other hand,

[1] Figures compiled by the National Industrial Conference Board apply to the year 1925.
[2] See Table XV, Statistical Information.

the average family income on St. Helena is only $420 per annum. An income as small as this is required in its entirety for food and clothing; it cannot be taxed by as much as a dollar without entailing severe hardship.

Nor is this $420 income on St. Helena entirely in cash. It includes food raised at home and an allowance for rent of an owned house. The cash income of seventy-five selected families studied in 1928 was only $270. Their income in cash and in kind, from farm operations, was $190. Their average tax bill was $11.73. This is an average tax payment of 4.3 per cent of the money income and 6.2 per cent of the income from farm operations.

Where the total amount of cash income is less than $300 per family, it is obvious that tax payments can be met only by economizing on daily bread. However, bread cast upon the waters may be found again, and taxes, even though wrung from the scanty and precarious livelihood of the poor, may, if properly expended, yield benefits which far outweigh the sacrifices involved. As has already been indicated, the chief grievance of the St. Helenites centers around the conviction that little of their tax bread returns to them in the form of governmental services. Rightly or wrongly, they feel that an undue proportion of their hard-earned money is expended for purposes which benefit other sections of the county than their own.

Superficially at least, there is considerable justification for this feeling. The casual observer sees little tangible evidence of the beneficial effects of governmental activity on St. Helena. With the exception of a fairly good dirt road from the middle of the Island to the town of Beau-

GOVERNMENT BENEFITS

fort, there are no improved roads in the township. Other so-called roads are mere wagon trails, stretches of which occasionally show traces of having at one time been surfaced with oyster shells. Some work was done in improving the main road through the center of the Island in the summer of 1927. Aside from this there are no indications of any attempt at road maintenance.

The county operates nine schools on the Island. All but two are one-room buildings and only one of the one-room schools is in good repair. In three of the schools the number of pupils per teacher is in excess of seventy-five, and in six it is in excess of fifty. The schools are operated from public funds for five months of the year only, and the average salary of the twelve teachers employed is $37 per month. The entire cost of running the schools of St. Helena for the school year 1927-28 was less than $2,500.[3]

Besides the schools and the small amount of road improvement work, the taxpayers of St. Helena receive very little direct return for their money. Beaufort County pays half of the salary and expenses of a colored farm demonstration agent, who makes his home on Ladies Island and devotes a large part of his time to the farmers of St. Helena. A drainage commission accumulates a few hundred dollars a year for the maintenance of the Island's drainage canals. A small number of paupers are furnished monthly doles, but the amount expended for this purpose in 1927 was less than two hundred dollars.

The monetary value of these services is shown in Table

[3] See Table XX, Statistical Information. After these tabulations were made, school appropriations in 1928-29 were increased to $2,850 for the district with a monthly teachers' salary averaging $41.

XVI, Statistical Information.[4] With the most liberal allowances, the full value of the governmental services which were of direct benefit to St. Helena have averaged less than $7,000 per year during the past seven years, and the taxes collected from the Island averaged about $16,500 per annum. In other words, the inhabitants of St. Helena receive back in direct governmental services about two-fifths of what they are obliged to contribute in taxes.

The foregoing figures indicate that the taxpayers of St. Helena receive very little direct return for their money. It requires further investigation to determine whether the other three-fifths are compensated for by indirect returns from the services of the county and the state. Fairness does not require that all tax monies collected on St. Helena be expended for the exclusive benefit of the Islanders. St. Helena is a part of the larger political units, the county and the state. These latter agencies carry on certain activities in the interest of their citizens as a whole.

It is the duty of St. Helena to support the functions of the larger political units of which it is a part. Where the functions in question are of county-wide, or of state-wide importance, it may even be right for St. Helena to contribute more in taxes than it receives back in direct local benefits. Justice requires, however, that two elementary rules be observed. First, St. Helena should be made to

[4] These monetary estimates err, if at all, on the side of liberality. For instance, they include all capital improvements, which normally do not recur as often as every seven years, such as the interest and amortization charges on the Beaufort-St. Helena bridge, which was not open to traffic until 1927, a new school building, the cost of all road work, including the purchase of machinery and establishment of a camp on the Island, and the full county quota of the demonstration agent's salary, although he spends part of the time in other districts than St. Helena.

GOVERNMENT BENEFITS 165

contribute no more, in proportion to its taxable capacity, than other localities within the same jurisdiction. Second, to the extent that the activities of the county and state give rise to measurable special benefits to particular localities, St. Helena's participation in such local benefits should be on a basis of equality with that of other localities whose relative contributions toward the common costs are no greater than its own. Whether or not these elementary rules are being observed is a question which can be answered only on the basis of a more detailed study of the specific governmental functions carried on in Beaufort County, with particular reference to the inter-local apportionment of the resulting benefits and burdens.

As everyone knows, the enormous outlay for highway development, which each year is becoming a greater strain on the financial resources of state and local governments, is a direct result of the revolution in transportation which came with the automobile. The revolution in question has, as yet, scarcely touched St. Helena. The prevailing mode of transportation is still represented by the horse-drawn vehicle. Even the primitive ox-cart has not yet disappeared, and it presents a picturesque sight as it zigzags its slow way along the deeply rutted, sandy roads. In 1927 only fifty-seven motor vehicles were listed for taxation by residents of St. Helena. Most of these were decrepit second-hand cars as is indicated by the fact that the combined taxable value of all fifty-seven vehicles was only $4,160.

It is obvious that St. Helena does not require an expensive highway system. Were the Island an independent political entity, it is extremely doubtful whether the inhabitants would consider it worthwhile to spend more than a few hundred dollars a year on the upkeep of their roads. Certainly they would not vote to tax themselves for motor highways, while 90 per cent of them are too poor to own even a second-hand flivver.

Despite their inability to derive much benefit from modern highways, the inhabitants of St. Helena have, during the last seven years, contributed some $44,000 toward the improvement of Beaufort County's roads. This sum is ten times greater than the assessed value of the Island's investment in motor cars and represents an average levy of $6,300 per year. Table XVII shows in detail the amounts of various highway taxes collected in St. Helena during the years 1921 to 1927 inclusive. It will be seen from this table that the Islanders are subject to three kinds of highway taxes. The most onerous of these exactions is the county-wide property levy for public roads. The rate of this tax has increased from $7\frac{1}{4}$ mills in 1921 to $13\frac{3}{4}$ mills in 1927. Its yield in St. Helena during the last seven years has averaged around $3,300 per annum. Next in point of burdensomeness is the capitation road tax, which, as previously indicated, is a poll tax of $3.50 on every able-bodied male between the ages of twenty-one and sixty. On the average, this tax exacts a tribute from the Islanders of some $2,250 per year. Finally, the townships of Beaufort and St. Helena are subject to a special tax to meet the interest and amortization charges on Beaufort-St. Helena bridge bonds. St. Helena's share of this expense during the last seven years has averaged around $730 per annum.

It has already been indicated that the county has spent only about $8,000 for road improvement on St. Helena for

GOVERNMENT BENEFITS 167

the years 1920 through 1927. All of this amount has been expended since the completion of the bridge in 1926. This was perhaps all that was necessary. The wagon trails which traverse the Island in all directions are well suited to the needs of the Negro farmers, and because of the sandy nature of the terrain these roads require little in the way of maintenance. All of St. Helena's contribution toward the county-wide property tax for public roads and the major portion of its payments under the capitation road tax were thus expended in other parts of the county.

There was nothing illegal about this disposition of St. Helena's road taxes. The property tax for public roads is levied at a uniform rate over the entire county. Its proceeds are spent on the county highway system, which, it is assumed, benefits the people of the county as a whole. Over half of it is required to meet debt service charges on county highway bonds. At the close of 1927 the county, as such, had a highway debt of $530,000. It also had some splendid highways, including thirty-three miles of concrete, thirty-six miles of gravel, and twenty-five miles of sand-clay road. If none of the improved roads traverse St. Helena, it is because St. Helena is not located on the main lines of traffic. If the St. Helenites, with their fifty-seven motor vehicles, are unable to extract much benefit from the motor highways which they are required to support, it is the penalty they have to pay for their poverty.

The capitation or commutation road tax is likewise a county-wide levy. The law directs that all funds collected under its provisions shall be used for general road purposes as set forth under Item 1 of the County Supply Act, and that "in so far as practicable there shall be expended in each Township an amount equal to the commutation tax collected in same Township." [5]

During the last seven years the county has expended considerably less on St. Helena's roads than the amount collected from the Island in commutation taxes. The difference has presumably been spent in other parts of the county. Although this diversion of the Islanders' tax monies may seem in the highest degree unjust, it can scarcely be attacked as illegal. The county officials might plausibly argue that the primitive methods of transportation still in use on the Island render it both unnecessary and impracticable to spend St. Helena's full quota of the commutation tax in improving the Island's roads. Any unexpended balance might, it is true, be applied toward reducing St. Helena's share of the debt service charges on the Beaufort-St. Helena bridge. To meet these charges, the township is now subject to a special property tax. Major projects such as the bridge are not, however, ordinarily included under Item 1 of the County Supply Act. The heavy tribute exacted from St. Helena in return for the illusory benefits of motor highways is thus strictly in accordance with law. The Island is simply the victim of its isolation, of its poverty, and of the fact that it is tied to a county whose dominant economic interests are at variance with its own.

The situation in which St. Helena finds itself is by no means unique. It is duplicated in thousands of other backward rural communities in all parts of the United States. The unfortunate plight of these communities is due in the main to three causes. In the first place, the excessive zeal

[5] Acts of 1922, No. 457.

GOVERNMENT BENEFITS 169

of interested groups has led to the launching of highway projects whose cost to the taxpayers is not only far in excess of any possible benefits to them, but is also out of all proportion to their economic resources. In the second place, improper bases have been employed for the purpose of distributing highway costs among the various classes of taxpayers. A third reason, applicable especially to Negro communities, is the lack of consideration given to these communities because they have no voice in electing the officials. All of these causes have operated to bring about the present situation in St. Helena.

That Beaufort County is spending more for highway development than its taxable resources would seem to warrant is indicated by a number of tests. In South Carolina as a whole in 1927 the amount of local taxes for schools was over three times as great as the amount of taxes levied for roads.[6] In Beaufort County, on the other hand, the aggregate amount of local road levies in 1927 was about 24 per cent greater than the total amount levied for schools. At the close of 1927 Beaufort County's total highway debt, including district bond issues, amounted to $696,800. This sum represented more than 17 per cent of the aggregate assessed wealth of the county. For the state as a whole, county and district highway indebtedness amounted to only 8 per cent of the total property assessment.[7] In 1927 there were 898 motor vehicles registered for taxation in the county. On a per vehicle basis the highway indebtedness was, therefore, $776 per car. The corresponding ratio for the state as a whole was only $274 per car.

[6] Report of the Comptroller General, 1927, p. 76.
[7] *Ibid.*, p. 82.

The increase in Beaufort County's highway indebtedness was undoubtedly facilitated by the fact that the state legislature could authorize county and district bond issues without first submitting the question to a vote of the taxpayers affected. With fewer than 900 motor vehicle owners in the county, it is doubtful whether the majority of the taxpayers would have voluntarily assumed the heavy highway burden they are now called upon to bear. Another important factor was the repeal, as regards Beaufort County, of the constitutional provision which limits the aggregate indebtedness of the county and its subordinate units to 15 per cent of the total property assessment. Had this limitation remained in effect, it would have somewhat reduced the volume of highway issues.

St. Helena's burdensome highway taxes are due in part to the overly ambitious construction program of the county authorities. They are also due in no small measure to the inequitable manner in which the county's highway costs are apportioned among the various classes of taxpayers. It is generally conceded that the principle of benefit should be given the broadest possible application in the financing of highways. In other words, highways should, as far as practicable, be paid for by the highway users, by owners of benefited property, and by the particular localities whose needs the highways are designed to serve. General taxation for highway purposes should be resorted to only after the possibilities of benefit taxation have been exhausted, and should be confined to projects which are in the interest of the taxpayers as a whole. Moreover, general taxes, levied without reference to special benefits received,

GOVERNMENT BENEFITS 171

should be apportioned among individual taxpayers strictly in accordance with their economic ability.

South Carolina applies the benefit principle to the taxation of highway users through the imposition of a gasoline sales tax of six cents per gallon, in the proceeds of which county governments are allowed to share. As far as Beaufort County is concerned, the application of the benefit principle stops here. Practically no attempt is made to distribute highway costs on the basis of township benefits. Interest and retirement charges on certain township bond issues are, it is true, financed on the basis of special township levies. All other highway expenditures, including all amounts spent for highway maintenance, are, however, financed on a county-wide basis, the general property and capitation taxes being used for this purpose. This means that township roads which benefit only restricted local areas are improved and maintained from funds collected from the county as a whole. If the amount spent on local highways in each township were in proportion to the amount of highway taxes collected from the township, there might be no injustice in such an arrangement. This is emphatically not the case as regards St. Helena. The amount spent on the maintenance of St. Helena's local roads is next to nothing. Yet of the eight school districts in the county, only two contribute more to the county's highway funds.

Central administration of all highway operations, including work on local roads, is undoubtedly in the interest of economy and efficiency. This does not require, however, that local roads be supported on a county-wide basis. If a sharper distinction were made between roads which are important to the county as a whole and roads which have merely a local value, and if county-wide support were strictly limited to the former class of roads, St. Helena's tax burden would be considerably reduced.

Further relief would come to the Island if the system of county-wide road taxes were made to conform more strictly with the principle of taxation according to ability. As has already been indicated, approximately two-fifths of the sum extracted from St. Helena for general highway purposes represents the yield of a capitation tax of $3.50 per head. This is a highly regressive tax, which bears much more heavily upon poor, thickly populated localities like St. Helena than it does upon the more affluent sections of the county. For individuals whose incomes reach to $2,000, which is the average income per family for the state as a whole, a capitation tax of $3.50 is equivalent to an income tax of less than one-sixth of one percent. In St. Helena, on the other hand, where the average cash income per family is less than $300, a capitation tax of $3.50 is equivalent to an income tax of $1\frac{1}{6}$ per cent. In other words, the capitation tax is seven times as burdensome to the St. Helenites as it is to individuals whose incomes equal the general state average. The capitation tax might be less objectionable, if its proceeds were spent on local roads in the immediate vicinity of the taxpayer's home. There is no justification, however, for using any part of it to support the general county highway system. Much less is it justifiable to spend capitation taxes collected in one township for the purpose of improving local roads situated in other townships.

GOVERNMENT BENEFITS 173

As has already been indicated, Beaufort County has financed an overwhelming proportion of its highway costs by means of county-wide taxes. St. Helena has been the chief sufferer from this practice, which has compelled it to share in the upkeep of purely local highways in other parts of the county. In financing the Beaufort-St. Helena bridge, however, the more usual policy of the county was reversed. The cost of this project was assessed against the two townships of Beaufort and St. Helena, presumably on the ground that these two townships received a special benefit. Whether this application of the benefit principle was legitimate, as regards St. Helena, may best be judged after a review of some of the more pertinent facts.

The town of Beaufort is something of a tourist resort. It is, however, located inland on the Beaufort River and lacks the attraction of ocean bathing. There are several desirable ocean-front beaches on smaller outlying islands which might be reached by way of St. Helena. A connection with these beaches by means of a modern motor highway would obviously increase Beaufort's attractiveness as a tourist center. It would also give the people of the mainland a chance to disport themselves in the surf.

The first step in the direction of establishing such a connection was the building of the bridge across the Beaufort River from Beaufort to Ladies Island. Although this bridge was not completed until 1927, the history of the project dates back to 1911. In that year the General Assembly passed an act to empower Beaufort and St. Helena townships to issue bonds for the purpose of building a bridge, and approaches, from the town of Beaufort to

Ladies Island, and to provide for the payment thereof.[8] The act in question provided for an election to be held in the two townships before the bonds should be issued. The election was duly held and the majority in St. Helena voted against the bonds. Beaufort Township, however, gave a majority in favor of the bonds, and since there were more voters in this township, the combined vote of both townships showed a majority in favor of the bonds.

The General Assembly chose to be guided by the results of the combined vote, and, disregarding the wishes of St. Helena, it passed an act in 1914 validating the election and authorizing work on the bridge to proceed. The St. Helena Township Commissioners thereupon instituted legal proceedings to enjoin the Beaufort County Commissioners from issuing the bonds on the ground that such issuance was unconstitutional. This action, however, proved unavailing. The Supreme Court of the state ruled that the General Assembly could have ordered the issuance of the bonds even without the formality of an election. It was pointed out that the legislature had the power to consolidate townships, either permanently or for a special purpose. Its action in combining the vote of Beaufort and St. Helena in connection with the bond election was, therefore, held to be perfectly legal.[9]

Bridge bonds to the amount of $80,000 were issued in 1921. The interest and retirement charges on these bonds are met by additions to the property tax rates of Beaufort and St. Helena townships. The additional rate has averaged around two mills per dollar.

[8] 27 *Stat. at Large*, p. 291.
[9] Fripp et al., Township Com'rs. v. Coburn et al., County Com'rs., 85 S. E. 774.

GOVERNMENT BENEFITS 175

With the completion of the bridge, plans were advanced for the building of a hard-surfaced road through St. Helena Township to one of the outlying beaches. The decision of the court in the bridge case having established the fact that St. Helena might be taxed to pay for a project which it did not want, it was first proposed to assess the entire cost of the road against that township. An act to this effect was passed at the 1926 session of the General Assembly.[10] This act authorized the Beaufort County Board of Commissioners to issue bonds of St. Helena Township up to an amount of $235,000 for the purpose of building the road. It is worth noting that the amount of bonds authorized was equivalent to approximately 50 per cent of the total assessed valuation of the township. The act directed that the bonds were not to be sold until private owners had donated to the county a tract of land of not less than one hundred acres fronting on the Atlantic Ocean. Apparently this stipulation was not fulfilled. At any rate the act never became effective, and it was repealed by the General Assembly of 1928.[11]

The project of a hard-surfaced road through St. Helena to the Atlantic Ocean has not, however, been abandoned. The legislature of 1928 passed another act which is somewhat less severe on St. Helena.[12] This act provides for the building of a road from the terminus of the Beaufort-St. Helena bridge to a point on the southern peninsula of St. Helena opposite Bay Point. Not more than $140,000 worth of bonds are to be issued to finance this road, and they are to be the joint obligation of three townships—

[10] Acts of 1926, No. 704.
[11] Acts of 1928, No. 805.
[12] Acts of 1928, No. 810.

Beaufort, Sheldon, and St. Helena. Moreover, issuance of the bonds is contingent upon the building of a private toll bridge connecting Bay Point with the southern terminus of the proposed road. No bonds are to be sold until work on the bridge has actually commenced and bond has been given to guarantee its completion.

A Northern capitalist owns property on Bay Point which he contemplates developing into a beach resort. The legislature has given him a franchise to build the proposed toll bridge from Bay Point to St. Helena.[13] According to the terms of the franchise actual construction of the bridge must begin on or before May 23, 1930. As yet no move has been made to build the bridge and the issuance of the $140,000 of township road bonds is, accordingly, being held in abeyance.

It is difficult to see what possible benefit can accrue to the Negro farmers of St. Helena as a result of the building of the proposed highway. The new beaches will not be for them. They do not need a hard-surfaced highway, the existing road being well suited to their present requirements. The new highway is scarcely likely to enhance the value of their land or to increase their earning power. Indubitably property in the vicinity of the projected beach development will rise in value, but this property is for the most part owned by a few non-resident speculators. To assess any part of the cost of the highway upon the farmers of St. Helena, through the device of a special district tax, would therefore seem to involve a gross abuse of the benefit principle.

[13] Acts of 1928, No. 808.

GOVERNMENT BENEFITS

In concluding the discussion of Beaufort County's highway policy, it may be worthwhile to summarize briefly the particular respects in which that policy works an injustice to the inhabitants of St. Helena.

1. The county authorities have indulged in an ambitious program of highway construction out of all proportion to the economic resources of the county. This program has been authorized by the General Assembly without submission to a vote of the taxpayers. The inhabitants of St. Helena derive no particular benefit from the new highways. They are nevertheless being forced to bear a heavy share of the costs.

2. Current highway expenditures in Beaufort County are financed on the basis of uniform county-wide taxes. No distinction, however, is made between roads which are important to the county as a whole and roads which benefit restricted local areas only. Failure to make this distinction results in the taxation of St. Helena for the purpose of improving purely local roads in other parts of the county.

3. The high capitation road tax bears more heavily on the poor people of St. Helena than it does on the wealthier residents of the county.

4. The taxpayers of St. Helena have been assessed with a share of the cost of the Beaufort-St. Helena bridge on the principle of special benefit, despite the fact that they voted against the project. On the basis of the same principle it is planned that they be made to contribute to the cost of the new highway to Bay Point, although they have practically nothing to gain from that improvement.

Taken as a whole, local governments in the United States spend more money on public education than they spend on any other single governmental activity. South Carolina offers no exception to this rule. The people of the state as a whole tax themselves three times as heavily for schools as they do for highways, which are the schools' strongest competitors for public funds. Unlike the rest of the state, Beaufort County taxes itself more heavily for highways than it does for schools. It has already been indicated that the aggregate amount of county-wide and district levies for roads assessed against the inhabitants of the county in 1927 was some 24 per cent greater than the corresponding levies for schools. As regards St. Helena at least, it is nevertheless true that adequate schools are much more necessary to the welfare of the inhabitants than are improved roads. The question of whether the Islanders are receiving as much as they are entitled to in the matter of educational services is, therefore, extremely important.

There are no white schools on St. Helena. The white school enrollment of the Island fluctuates between twenty-five and thirty pupils, and these pupils are transported daily by motor bus to the Beaufort Town School. As will be seen from Table XVIII, the total enrollment of the Negro schools in 1927-28 was 688 pupils. Nine Negro schools were maintained. All but two of these were of the ungraded, one-teacher variety. Three of the ungraded schools had an enrollment in excess of seventy-five pupils per teacher. In other words, the teachers in these schools had the hopeless task of attempting to give instruction to seventy-five pupils of different grades and ages. The schools of St. Helena are operated from public funds for five months of the year only. The cost of operating them in 1927-28 was less than $2,500. Practically all of this sum represented teachers' salaries.

Reference has already been made to the fact that the school district has been virtually abandoned as an independent financial unit in Beaufort County. Since 1925 the county has financed all of its schools on the basis of county-wide taxes. The chief source of school revenue is a county-wide property tax of $14\frac{1}{2}$ mills. Seven mills levied by the state plus $7\frac{1}{2}$ mills levied by the county. The county also receives a considerable amount of financial support from a fund appropriated by the General Assembly for the purpose of equalizing educational opportunity throughout the state. Aid from the state, however, is limited to schools which comply with certain minimum requirements. In Beaufort County it is the County Board of Education which determines whether any particular school shall be accorded sufficient support from county funds to enable it to meet these minima. The schools of St. Helena receive no benefit from state aid, although the inhabitants of the Island contribute some $2,400 per year in state property taxes.

The farmers of St. Helena are subject to the same relative burden for schools as are other inhabitants of Beaufort County. They are subject to the same taxes at identical rates of levy. Equality in the matter of school burdens should logically entitle them to equality in the matter of educational services. That they are far from receiving this measure of justice is abundantly indicated by the data set forth in Table XIX. It will be seen from this table that the total cost of operating the schools of St. Helena in 1927-28 represented an expenditure by the county of only $3.36 per pupil enrolled. The corresponding averages for the county as a whole were $56 per pupil for the white schools, and $6.11 per pupil for the Negro schools. The St. Helena schools had an average session of 100 days as compared with an average session of 178 days for the white schools of the county as a whole, and an average session of 117 days for the Negro schools. The average annual salary of public school teachers on the Island was $185. For the county as a whole, the average salary of white teachers was $1,004, while the average for Negro teachers was $259 per annum. Finally, only one teacher was employed on the Island to every 57 school children enrolled. For the county as a whole the number of pupils per teacher was 26 for the white schools and 46 for the Negro schools.

It is evident that the school authorities of Beaufort County do not consider that equality in the matter of school tax burdens necessarily involves the obligation to equalize educational opportunities. This point of view cannot be condemned off-hand, if equal educational opportunity is to be understood as meaning the establishment of common standards for Negro and white schools. The Negroes of Beaufort County do not possess enough taxable wealth to support their schools according to white standards. If such standards were to be maintained, the additional cost would have to be defrayed by the white taxpayers. Beaufort County is not overly wealthy, and it is having a difficult struggle to maintain even its white schools in accordance with acceptable standards. These standards would be jeopardized if equal money were expended on Negro schools. Equality of educational opportunity as between Negroes and whites would, therefore, require a degree of altruism on the part of the white population which it is scarcely practical to expect. Under the circumstances, probably all that can be asked on behalf of the Negroes is that they receive back in school services at least as much as they contribute in school taxes, and that no part of their tax monies be used for the support of the white schools.

A significant fact brought out by Table XX is the relatively large and increasing amount spent on the handful of white children residing on the Island. The total expenditure for white children in 1927-28 amounted to more than half of what was spent on the 688 Negro children. Despite the liberal provision made for white children, it will be seen that the total current expenditure for education in St. Helena has fallen considerably short of the amount collected in school taxes during every one of the four years under review. Taking the period as a whole, less than two-thirds of the total taxes collected were actually expended on the Island for current school purposes. It is scarcely proper to charge all of the expense incident to the building of the Rosenwald School against the tax collections of a four-year period. New schools are a species of rarity on the Island which come with considerably less frequency than every four years. Even with the addition of this item, however, it will be seen that the total school expenditures for the four years under review amount to less than 77 per cent of the total school-tax collections.

It may be concluded that the taxpayers of St. Helena

are being made to contribute toward the education of the children of the rest of the county. Corroborative evidence of this fact is supplied from another source. In 1924 the schools of Beaufort County were still financed on the old district basis. In that year the town of Beaufort, the wealthiest school district in the county, had a district rate of 10 mills for current school maintenance. Two other districts had local school rates of 6 mills. Four districts, including St. Helena Island, had local school tax rates of only 4 mills. With the adoption of the county-wide basis of financing in 1925, a uniform rate of taxation for current school maintenance of $7\frac{1}{2}$ mills was put into effect. The school rate in the town of Beaufort was thus reduced by $2\frac{1}{2}$ mills. The rate of taxation in all the other districts was increased, St. Helena being saddled with an additional burden of $3\frac{1}{2}$ mills. There is no evidence that the reduction of school taxes in the town of Beaufort was accompanied by a corresponding reduction in educational expenditures for that district. As far as St. Helena is concerned, there is no evidence that the increase in its school tax rate was followed by a commensurate improvement in the quality of the educational offering. Obviously the relatively wealthy town of Beaufort was the chief gainer from the shift to the county-wide basis of taxation.

Public school administrators throughout the country are urging that the school district be abandoned in favor of the county as the financial unit for school support. It is contended that a broader tax base will tend to equalize educational opportunities and financial burdens by placing the resources of the richer communities at the disposal of the poorer ones. The fact that the adoption of a county-wide system of school support had quite the opposite effect in Beaufort County does not invalidate this argument. Beaufort's experience merely illustrates the danger of adopting a uniform county-wide system of school taxation without providing at the same time for uniform county-wide standards of educational performance. In the absence of such standards a broadening of the tax base may readily be made to lend itself to inter-district discrimination.

The data presented in the foregoing pages plainly indicate that St. Helena is a victim of such discrimination. It bears the same relative burden for schools as do other parts of the county. Nevertheless the educational opportunity offered its children is far below the average for the county as a whole. It may not be practicable, in view of the small amount of taxable wealth possessed by the Negroes, to give them the same educational advantages as those enjoyed by the whites. They are entitled at the very least, however, to the full value of their actual tax contribution, and it does not appear that the inhabitants of St. Helena are receiving even this minimum of consideration.

Undoubtedly the inhabitants of St. Helena have a real tax grievance. The evidence presented clearly shows that the Island has been discriminated against both in the matter of highways and schools. In fairness to the county authorities, however, it may be well, before concluding the study, to emphasize certain facts concerning the nature of this discrimination. In the first place, however reprehensible it may seem from the standpoint of abstract justice, the discrimination in question is not in any sense illegal. In the second place, the inequalities from which St. Helena suffers are not confined to any particular race. White communities, in the same situation as St. Helena, may be and probably are the victims of similar kinds of injustice; but when once aroused to the situation these communities have redress at the polls which is denied to Negro communities.

St. Helena's difficulties are in the final analysis traceable to certain defects of governmental organization. The lack of any constitutional restriction on the power of the General Assembly to authorize local tax levies and bond issues opens the way for interested parties, capable of influencing the county legislative delegation, to put through projects of very doubtful value to the taxpayers who are required to foot the bill. The indiscriminate use of the county-wide basis of taxation, without adequate provisions for safeguarding the interests of particular communities, makes inter-local favoritism in the expenditure of county funds a comparatively easy matter. To remedy the defects mentioned, it would be necessary to make fundamental changes in the constitution and statutory law of the state.

Relief for St. Helena need not, however, await the adoption of such changes. Although the treatment meted out to the Island is permitted under existing laws, it is by no means prescribed by them. There is nothing to prevent the authorities of Beaufort County from apportioning the benefits and burdens of local government in a fair and impartial manner. An awakening on the part of the dominant interests in the county to the real needs of its backward rural communities and a more sympathetic consideration of their interests are perhaps all that is needed to solve St. Helena's tax problem.

CHAPTER IX

EDUCATION

*I know I would like to read,
Like to read,
Like to read dat sweet story ob old.
I would like to read.*

Since emancipation, education has been a fetish of the freedmen, especially of the Islanders. Northern teachers came to St. Helena with the Northern troops and immediately schools were opened. The ex-slaves turned to books as a symbol of the culture of their former masters. In their eagerness to learn they filled the schools with pupils of all ages.

It is pathetic to see a whole community, old and young, put such blind faith in education. This, however, is merely an intensification of the American faith in schools as summed up by Professor Giddings, "We believe in education. Our faith in it is as unquestioning as the faith of primitive man in magic. And why not? Is not education descended from magic in the direct male line? . . . Why then should we think ill of ourselves if we have expected education to work miracles?" The elementary schools of the freedmen did not immediately give them a full grasp of American culture but eventually there came to St. Helena educators whose conception of the process was not magical, those who saw in the school a tool for fashioning lives rather than learning formulæ.

EDUCATION

The struggle to learn still continues. Children go through great hardships to get learning and their parents make great sacrifices. The family budget is pinched to supply tuition, books and clothes. Some children walk eight and ten miles, crossing bogs, and woods to attend.

Probably no group of rural Negroes in the world is more "literate" according to census standards [1] than the Islanders. More than 80 per cent of those over six years of age report some schooling. Half of these, however, never progressed beyond the third grade and though counted "literate" by the census have made little use of their training. Another 38 per cent finished the fourth or fifth grade and about one-eighth have been beyond the sixth grade.

The facilities for learning are far and way above those of the other Negro rural districts of the South. The public schools provided from taxation are slightly below the average but the program of that exceptional institution, Penn School, provides education which is a real process of training and character building. The results of this school have been so significant that hundreds of visitors from America and even from the mission stations and government houses of far-off Africa come to observe and analyze its activities in enriching rural community life.

When it is said that the public schools are near the average of Southern Negro communities, little enough has been implied. The schools of the Island share all the defects of the other rural schools. The term is short.

[1] The census merely asks whether a person can read and write, not whether they *actually do* read and write with any frequency.

Schools are so far apart that long distances over poor roads must be traversed by younger children. Teachers are poorly paid and buildings are crowded and in bad repair.

The county has wasted no money on the operation of the schools of the district. On the contrary it appears, from a view of the evidence in the chapter on taxation, that St. Helena has been taxed to support the schools in other parts of the county. County taxes of about $5,200 were paid in educational levies from the school district, of which $2,700, or about half, came back in annual appropriations for the Negro pupils of the district (Table XX). In addition an annual average of $735 is spent for transportation of the white pupils of the township to Beaufort schools. Thus the Islanders not only fail to get back what they pay in county levies, but also fail to share in the state subsidies apportioned from the state levies. This niggardly policy of the county board gives them a per capita annual expenditure of $3.36 per colored pupil as against $6.11 for the colored pupils of Beaufort County and $56 for white pupils of the county.

There has been only one public expenditure for school buildings in sixty years. This was the recent sharing by the county and state in the erection of a Rosenwald School. The greater part of the cost of this school was borne by private funds and the donations of the Islanders. In the past most of the island schools were erected and kept in repair from a fund of about $1,800 which was established by the sale of school lands designated by the Government for the use of the schools of St. Helena and St. Luke Parishes. But this fund no longer comes to the township since it has been thrown into the general county educational

EDUCATION

funds. Thus another financial injustice has been done to the public schools of the township.

Schools operate from public funds only five months in a year or 100 days. Parents and patrons of each school, however, pay from their scanty means a tuition of fifty cents per pupil for the extension of the term for a sixth month so that the full term is 120 days as against a state average of 117 days in South Carolina Negro schools. Thus the island public school children have only two-thirds of the normal time for learning.

The buildings of three of the nine schools are in good repair and the other six are very dilapidated. All but two are one-room structures and very crowded. Three schools have been closed because the buildings were destroyed by wind or fire. Only the new Rosenwald School has patent desks and blackboards. The others have stiff hand-made benches inadequate in number. Makeshift blackboards are the only teaching equipment. Most of the rooms are so crowded as to render teaching very difficult. Several average more than seventy-five pupils per teacher. (Table XVIII.) And in these schools the pupils are jammed all the way from wall to wall and from the teacher to the doorstep. There have been times in recent years when a school would become so over-run that the maximum number would be packed in and then the teacher would close the doors and tell the late arrivals they would have to go home.

Several of these one-teacher schools should be expanded to care for the excess of pupils. One or two could be consolidated, but the majority now serve such a large area that, without transportation, further consolidation would not be possible. An additional obstacle to consolidation is that some of the schools are located on peninsulas extending five or six miles out from the main part of the Island, so that if these schools were moved inland, children would have to walk the length of the peninsula.

An unusually high proportion (80 per cent) of the children six to sixteen are in school. Of these, slightly over two-thirds are in the public schools, and less than one-third in Penn School. The attendance of many in the schools is exceedingly irregular because those who live far away are kept away by heavy rains or kept at home to attend to farm chores.

It is not to be expected that a good teacher can be obtained for the salary of $145 a year. Nevertheless, Penn School is able to persuade some of its graduates to stay and teach in the public school through a spirit of service. In addition to the low salary scale, the teachers have the difficulty of teaching in overcrowded rooms, of handling ungraded pupils who attend irregularly and who attempt to learn without possessing a book. Much of the recitation, therefore, is in concert and a great deal of the time is taken up with singing spirituals and telling the animal stories that the Islanders love so much.

Under this situation learning is a discouraging process. Nevertheless in the public schools many manage to get through the readers after a fashion, to learn to write a little and to become familiar with elementary education. On the other hand, some become so retarded that they get discouraged and quit. However, as has been said, 80 per cent of those from six to sixteen are in school.

ROSENWALD SCHOOL

SCHOOL GARDENING

EDUCATION

It was discovered that three little boys had been in school three years and were still in the first grade. This was surprising since they seemed to be rather bright children. When they were questioned it was learned that their parents had never taken the time or trouble to go to Beaufort to buy them a book. But when books were bought for them and they came down at night for about an hour's individual instruction, they all managed to master the first reader and the smaller multiplication tables and to begin to write in four months. When they first started reading, they seemed to be excellent scholars, but it was soon discovered that they had heard the stories read in class so many times that they knew them by heart and could recite them correctly when they saw the picture on the page. They did not, however, know one word from the other when they were not in regular order. This is a sample of the education in one of the poorer public schools.

The future of the public schools is not so dark. One Rosenwald School has already been built and, under the leadership of Penn School, the whole Island has been districted and a program launched for building these schools in each district.

In the Rosenwald School, the district has an example of the movement which has done so much toward improving Negro schools all over the South. Thousands of better school buildings have been scattered through the rural districts, and the quality of teaching has been greatly improved, through the generosity of Mr. Rosenwald's offer to meet a good proportion of the cost of a modern rural school building on condition that the balance is paid by the county or from local subscriptions and that the county agrees to supply funds for satisfactory annual maintenance.

The one Rosenwald School in the district, erected two years ago, is a marked contrast to the other public schools. It is a three-teacher graded school with a modern well-lighted building, good equipment, and comfortable seating arrangements. Owing to the requirements which must be met to secure the Rosenwald donation, the teachers are better paid and better qualified for their work.

As this report is written, the Rosenwald Fund has announced its willingness to participate in a Island-wide program of building similar schools and the people are contributing, from their limited incomes, money to meet their share of the cost. So that as rapidly as the county officials are able to do their part, the schools all over the Island can be improved.

The spirit of cooperation of the people in building these schools is worthy of note. The contribution of $500 raised locally for the present school was not secured from the patrons of that school alone, but was contributed by an Island-wide campaign and it is planned to erect the other schools in the same way so that each new school will be a contribution from the whole Island instead of merely from the people of one neighborhood.

Another progressive feature in Negro education, which is exemplified in the district, is the supervising teacher. In several hundred counties of the South, the Anna T. Jeanes Fund appropriates part of the salary of the teacher whose responsibility is county-wide rather than for just one school. She travels from school to school encouraging the local teachers and helping them to meet their everyday problems from a fund of experience which is broader than that of the young rural teacher. Penn School employs such a supervising teacher on its staff to visit the public schools, to assist the local teachers, and to organize the parents. Thus its educational program is not only concerned with its own pupils but includes a vital interest in the development of the public schools of the Island.

The real educational opportunity of the Island is, however, not in the public schools, but in Penn Normal Industrial and Agricultural School,[2] the oldest Negro school in the South. Its program has expanded to include both a broad type of training and of character building for its pupils, and a wise leadership and stimulation of all the essential activities of the community.

Historically, Penn School is the outgrowth of a missionary interest manifested in the North, during and immediately after the Civil War. The experiences of the early missionary workers who followed the Union troops to the Island were instrumental in shaping the policies of the Freedmen's Bureau in its early educational efforts and those of the church Mission Boards in planning their activities for Negro education.

It was founded by Miss Laura M. Towne, who came down from Philadelphia to begin the work in 1862. With her assistant, Miss Ellen Murray, she carried on the work until 1905, when they retired and the management was taken over by Miss Rossa B. Cooley and Miss Grace B.

[2] Statistics of Penn School are given in Table XXI, Appendix.

House,[3] two former teachers at Hampton Institute. At this time Dr. Hollis B. Frissell, then the principal of Hampton, assumed the position as head of the Board of Trustees of Penn School, and the institution which had gained the confidence and respect of the Islanders as a rather thorough school of traditional standards became an agricultural school with activities extending throughout the whole community and ideals of education as broad as life itself, an institution whose work is so striking as to cause a visiting colonial educator from Africa to regard it as the most significant thing which he saw upon his visit to America.

In Penn School private funds and interest have taken up the task of education where public funds fell short. On its Board of Trustees, it has included educators of the type of Dr. Frissell, several representatives of the group of northern philanthropists who have, for a half century, supported Negro educational institutions, and several prominent South Carolinians who represent the most favorable traditions of the South. This organization has placed Penn School among a number of private institutions which have preserved a very necessary contact between white people and Negroes. The bitterness of reconstruction, and segregation tendencies, threw Negroes too much on their own resources, isolated them too much. Such schools, however, were a vital link between their life and white culture.

The pupils come from all over the Island and a few from other parts of the tide-water country. A small boarding department cares for these off-island pupils and for some

[3] With Miss Cooley came Miss Frances Butler, who died after a month on the Island. Her place was taken by Miss House.

EDUCATION

who live on the Island. It is the policy of the school to keep the older pupils in residence for at least a year before they graduate.

A quarter of the children from six to sixteen years of age are enrolled in Penn School. A nominal tuition of $5 is something of a selective force and special effort is made by the management to encourage the better-prepared and more ambitious children from the public schools.

"Far-away" children, who formerly had to make a round trip of sixteen and eighteen miles on foot over rough roads and across marshy stretches, now have their journey shortened by busses, "chariots," operated by the school.

Many of the teachers are Islanders, Penn School graduates, who have gone on to Hampton for further training. They are efficient and faithful. The most remarkable characteristic of the staff is its cooperative spirit. Teachers of class room subjects go out during planting week and visit the agricultural and gardening projects. Industrial teachers are interested in the class room instruction and each member of the staff seems aware of all activities of the school, rather than of their own particular job. This spirit of cooperation is especially manifest among the full time community workers. The farm demonstration agent is active in bettering the homes and the home demonstration agent gives intelligent advice on better gardens, and both are promoting pure bred poultry. Both of these workers are prominent in health movements and the nurse reenforces the economic program of the demonstration agents. Cooperating in this manner, the total effectiveness of the working force is greater than the usual efforts of social workers to improve different phases of community life through highly specialized and uncoordinated activity.

Cooperative spirit and cooperative action is renewed and given intelligent guidance through the "Community Council" organized by the school. In this organization the teachers, the community workers, the preachers and the doctor discuss the constructive activities.

The educational values of the school are as much in the intangible qualities of the instruction as they are in the studies and industries which are formally scheduled. These intangible qualities are rooted in the relation of the teaching to the realities of life in many subtle ways. Both the class room and the industrial subjects are continually adapted to community needs. Arithmetic is taught in relation to household problems or methods of land estimation. Pupils participate in industrial work not only to become skilled, but also to cultivate the fundamental habits of thoroughness and morality which are best formed by doing tasks well.

The class room subjects extend from the first through the eleventh grade. This program falls short of the standard course required for a high school graduate's teacher's certificate by the omission of foreign languages. However, it adds more thorough training in industry than is possible in public schools.

The term of instruction is harmonized with the life of the community. In the spring, pupils are dismissed for "planting week" and teachers visit them at home instead of in the class room. From then on school is suspended each Friday for pupils to work on the home farm. With these holidays and the time taken from class room work to learn industries and agriculture, it is necessary to operate the school during the summer in order to cover, in one year, the usual graded subjects. With the exception of short recesses in the spring and fall the term is continuous.

All pupils take agriculture and in addition each is given a knowledge of the use of the tools and the fundamental processes in one of the shops. The industries are well equipped. The industries are: Wheelwrighting, carpentry, blacksmithing, cobbling and harness making, and basketry for boys, cooking and sewing teacher training for girls. For rural life manual proficiency in these lines is invaluable.

The boys' industries are housed in well-equipped shops with a trained tradesman in charge of each. In addition to instructing the pupils, the industries serve the community. Carts are brought to be mended in the wheelwright department. Shoes and harness are renovated. Rope and string are replaced by leather. Thus along with the buzz of the class room goes the ring of the hammer and whir of machinery.

The girls' homemaking activities are carried on in a typical five-room house erected on the school grounds by the carpentry department and furnished by the girls. Thorough instruction in cooking and sewing with actual practice in caring for the house is included. The cooking department gives practical lessons in canning as well as in the planning and preparation of meals. In the sewing classes the girls make a number of things for sale as well as for their own home. Costumes for plays and their own graduation dresses furnish practical lessons in needlework. Before completing the course all articles of clothing including a baby's layette are made. Mending is as important a part of the work as making new articles.

A most valuable activity of the cooking department is the planning and preparation of from 75 to 100 school lunches each day, for sale to the pupils at 3 and 5 cents each. By this system, children are saved a long wait for lunch and those from the poorer homes are greatly benefited by the wholesome meal. Spindle shanks fill out and young bodies are rounded after a few months of at least one good meal a day.

The school farm has made steady progress in usefulness. The 1925 catalog contains the following summary of its growth:

"From one blind horse, a shed for a barn, one wagon, one small plow, when work started on the School Farm of 70 acres in 1904, we had added in 1916, 50 acres of land, 2 mules, 2 horses, a good sized barn, a silo, a small sugarcane mill, 3 cows, a few hogs, and some poultry. Farm tools had made it possible to cultivate 49 acres in food and general farm crops.

"In 1924 the farm had increased to 276 acres. The equipment on the farm included a new dairy barn and milk house, a tractor, 4 mules, a pure bred Guernsey bull, a herd of 7 cows, a small poultry plant of pure Rhode Island Reds, and a herd of pure bred Duroc Jersey hogs." In 1929 a commodious new barn was added.

The school farm is an experiment and demonstration station. New crops are tried and methods of getting larger yields of familiar crops worked out. Demonstrations in poultry and dairying accompany lessons in field crops.

The calves, named Easter, April and May, are as much a part of the school equipment as the blackboards.

Agricultural instruction is given in two places. Tasks are assigned on the school farm and each pupil is encouraged to cultivate a home acre which is regularly visited by the teachers. Thus the whole community is an agricultural class room.

The character-building value of such productive work, well supervised, is apparent in the following letter about a boy's farm duties:

Please see to this, if we don't do any thing else, we must send our plow horses into the fields with tight harness, no strings, no wires, no broken pieces. Our driving harness must be kept in repair, I was sent a horse the other day with the bridle tied in a knot instead of being fixed with a buckle. This will not do for Penn School with a harness shop. Then too I don't think ——— ever thinks of washing a buggy or harness unless he is told to do it.

We can't go on like this. I am writing this because I have talked and advised with him a great deal since November about this very work. We must have these things attended to. No wires, no strings, no knots, in or on any of the harness, and our harness ready for inspection at any time. This is ———'s job to attend to these things at the barn while you are out over the rest of the farm. Now Mr. ——— must show some improvement along these lines, we can't go any longer like this.

Please read this to him and see if you can do anything to make these things right.

It is in character as well as in knowledge and skill that the results of this program show.

It has already been noted that the standard of living

of the people is considerably improved by such training. They get some of the habits of work which enable them to produce—habits taught former generations by slavery. They learn things which enable them to make more of what they have. The household arts of the girls and the carpentry of the boys make better homes without recourse to hired labor. The manual training enables the men to do dozens of odd farm jobs of repair. It is not so generally understood, however, that even for the industrial life of the city, such training and character building is as valuable as any current type of education. Penn School students are able to cope with life whether they stay at home or move to the city. In the endeavor to see just what place in city life is taken by the graduates and ex-students many of them were visited in their city homes. There are two doctors, a number of teachers, some business men and housekeepers of good homes. Most of them are well up in the scale of city dwellers. Thus the school meets the test of preparation for and stimulation to a fuller life whether it be in the city or in the country.

As the urbanization of the Negro proceeds their schools are confronted more and more with the double task of preparing some pupils for rural life, and giving the others a sound foundation to build upon if they move to the city. At the present rate of movement, rural schools are forced to train two pupils for each one who stays in the community.

Over and above the instruction of pupils, this institution has tremendous significance as a force throughout the community. It permeates all the activities of the Island. The program centers in a beautiful community house. When

EDUCATION 201

one sees this house with the library, the sewing classes, the midwives' class, the community sings and the "movies," all enthusiastically attended, one wonders how it is possible that other rural schools get along with a community house.

The outstanding neighborhood activities have been described elsewhere, but at the risk of repetition they are summarized here again so that their range and scope may be visualized.[4]

Chronologically they begin before birth with prenatal instruction to mothers by the school nurse. Infants come in for baby day when normal weight babies are pridefully awarded blue ribbons. And any community which can assemble out of 130 newly born a group of from twenty-five to thirty-five blue ribbon babies annually is staging an event of great future significance. From then on the activities extend to the autumn of life when the mothers and grandmothers of from sixty to eighty are assembled in the community class to quilt and sew, sing and gossip.[5]

Breadwinning is approached through the work of the farm demonstration agent in crop improvement and animal breeding. It is vividly discussed at the annual farmers' fair where competition not only includes the exhibits of crops and livestock, but also the effort to tell the most interesting story of a year's progress in the "experience meeting," a keenly anticipated feature.

Homemaking is stimulated by the canning clubs and homemakers' groups of the home demonstration agent and culminates in the better home week when well-planned

[4] A list of the activities from the 1925 Catalog of Penn School is given in the Section on Statistical Information.
[5] See Appendix for full list of community activities of Penn School.

demonstrations attract island-wide attention, and stir ambitions to add a room here, a porch there, and yonder a coat of paint or a sanitary privy.

Health is attacked all along the line through the activities of the nurse and through cooperation with the community and State Health Department in vaccination, inoculation, sanitation and special preventive work against tuberculosis.

The surrounding public schools are improved through the activities of a visiting teacher, and leadership in securing funds and the land for improved Rosenwald School buildings. The Community House is open for meetings of public school teachers and patrons; and the public schools participate in the annual fair.

Recreational life is enriched by community sings, pageants, school entertainments and picnics. Before the school devoted attention to the lighter side of life, island children hardly knew how to play. In Miss Cooley's words:

"Farm life on St. Helena left little time for play, and play was not known in its true sense and value. There was loafing during 'off time,' and while there was baseball, which too often broke up in a quarrel, and one ring game, 'Little Sallie Water,' that was all.

"Folk games came, and children began to carry them home; other games have followed; school teams in baseball and basketball for boys and girls and football for boys have developed a spirit of real sportsmanship.

"The playground equipment at Penn School is continually being worn out through constant use, and children have been seen at 'dayclean' and in the moonlight using

EDUCATION 203

the swings. In the Penn School children there is a thorough awakening of the play spirit.

"Picnics and hikes have been introduced through the clubs, the Y.W.C.A. and the Y.M.C.A. Two plays on Better Homes were written and given by the children last year.

"Until more is done to provide recreation the occasional excursion to Savannah will continue to be patronized by hundreds. It has become a great social event in the monotonous year, and nothing yet takes its place. The social side of the people is now being reached through the regular meetings of the sewing circle, poultry club, canning clubs, community class, and the monthly society and lodge meetings."

Education of this type, especially when it includes industrial training and so many community activities, is relatively more expensive than the simple teaching of the three R's. This is the one chief reason why industrial and agricultural education has made so little headway in Southern rural districts. The financial backers of Penn School deserve especial credit for showing their faith in this type of education by substantial contributions. The educational budget [6] of the School is $44,000 per annum. With the exception of $6,000 for endowment, it is met by contributors well scattered over the country. The plant is valued at $154,000. It costs approximately $30,000 more per year to operate Penn School as a community center than if it were only a rural elementary and high school.

Thus we have applied four essential tests to the contacts of the school both with its pupils and with the adult mem-

[6] Excluding receipt from fees and shop sales—amounting to $6,200.

bers of its community. Does it make for better health? Does it aid in the transmission to the succeeding generation of heritage, physical and mental? Does it develop sound habits and skills in breadwinning? Does it enrich the spiritual and recreational life of the people? In the light of the full program which has been elaborated, the answers to all four of these questions is in the affirmative.

PUBLIC SCHOOL, EXTERIOR AND INTERIOR

CHAPTER X

THE HOME

I look all around me,
It look so shine,
I ask de Lord
If all were mine.

Marriage is a solemn affair with the Islanders. The young couple sometimes stand for an hour or an hour and a quarter before the minister while he reads a line or two from the ceremony and intersperses the lines with a lengthy lecture, jocose at times, but with a vein of seriousness running throughout.

"Do you, ——, tek dis woman for your lawful wedded wife?"

"I do."

"W'en you say you tek her, mean it. Look how purty she is. Keep her dat way. Worrin' about men meks women ugly. Keep tellin' her she's purty. Praise her cookin', doan come in and slam your hat down and say, 'Is dat all de vittles you got fer supper?'"

"Do you, ——, tek dis man fer your lawful wedded husband?"

"I do."

"Well, keep him den. Doan always be naggin'. A naggin' woman is a scourge on eart'. Doan lissen to all de tales everybody be tellin' you about him. Dere's always somebody to come around and scandalize de neighbors. Show him you trust him and he'll do right.

"Young man, where 'd you git de money to buy a nice ring like dis? Young woman, you see how nice it is. It shows how much he loves you. Keep it safe. Young man, always give her nice presents like dat."

Through all this and much more the groom fidgets, the bride looks down at her white gloves, the bride's mother adheres to convention by sniffling a little, and the two fathers look proud and relieved. When it is over there is no room to doubt that the preacher has done his best to see that the couple are thoroughly married.

Before the ordeal of the ceremony the bride has been dressed by her special friends. This takes from an hour and a half to two hours. The guests have slowly gathered, uninvited, for invitations are a matter of course. The relatives and immediate friends pack the room where the ceremony is held, and the neighbors and the curious fill the rest of the downstairs of the small house and overflow into the yard.

After the ceremony the guests stay around late consuming much cake and sometimes a little "vine" and indulging in banter and gossip. Then the young couple moves off down the road to an unoccupied piece of land belonging to some absent relative and the new home is started.

This comes after a conventional courting which follows the customs usually prevailing in the country. There are walks home from church, meetings at the store, a few parties, sitting up, but not late sitting, for work begins early on the farm, and shy hand holding as the young folks

THE HOME

walk home from the praise house down the inky black roads.

That the courting is not always so conventional is indicated by the fact that 30 per cent of the births are illegitimate (around forty per year). One reason why this percentage is high is that here the knowledge of contraceptive methods, seemingly so prevalent among modern youth, is totally lacking. Many of these couples marry afterwards, so that the problem is not so great as the figures might indicate. Sex irregularity after marriage is, however, not noticeable. The social pressure toward sex morality is applied by the church. Offenders are regularly turned out after a session with the deacons. They may get back in, however, after a due course of repentance.

After marriage most of these families stick together, except when one parent dies. About 57 per cent of the island families were headed by couples living together, 29 per cent by widows, 7 per cent by widowers, and 7 per cent by separated couples and older children of orphan families. (Table XXIII.) Divorce is not legal on any grounds in South Carolina so that most of those who separate merely quit, the man usually moving to the city to seek more congenial surroundings. The great excess of widows over widowers (332 to 86) is interesting and undoubtedly means that a few of those returning themselves as widows are really deserted. The excess, however, is largely owing to the greater tendency of widowers to remarry. It is also significant that two-thirds of the widows and only half of the widowers have children in their household.

Expressed in terms of the whole population over fifteen years of age, instead of in terms of heads of families, we find that among the women 55 per cent are married, 19 per cent single, and 24 per cent widowed. This is a lower percentage in both the married and the single groups and a higher percentage in the widowed group than is found in the whole Negro population or in the native white rural population. In other words, girls on the Island marry earlier, but more often remain widowed than those in the whole Negro population or in the white rural population. Most of the single women are between fifteen and twenty-five. Only a small number of women over twenty-five are unmarried. Old maids are practically unknown. Of the married women, 35 per cent are married by the age of seventeen, 76 per cent by twenty, and 94 per cent by twenty-five. Among the males, 23 per cent are single, 68 per cent are married and 9 per cent widowers. There is a much smaller proportion of single males in the St. Helena population than in either the whole Negro population or the white rural population and the proportion of married and widowers is slightly larger. (Table XXIV.)

There is no career on the Island which does not have yeoman agriculture and the yeoman family as its basis and those desiring other careers do not fit into the picture. They must go elsewhere.

The prevalence of old widows was spoken of in the chapter on population as one of the results of the draining off of males by migration. Few of the old widows live alone, however. Miss Cooley says,[1] "It is rather unusual to find the old women living alone. There is usually a

---
[1] *Homes of the Freed*, p. 101.

'grand' who can be spared or a 'mudderless' who can be adopted. We shall never forget Aunt Riah and Husky. Two most pathetic figures they were—Aunt Riah somewhere about ninety, and Husky somewhere about ten. They came to school from their little old house on Frogmore, a walk of about three miles, and we always wondered how they managed it. Aunt Riah looked older than anyone I have ever seen, and Husky, hollow-eyed and with the thinnest legs on St. Helena, had surely outgrown his name. He had been a 'mudderless' and Aunt Riah had taken him in." It is thus that the women, especially the old women, bear the load imposed on them by migration.

Some of the older of these 332 widows are in straits which, in other communities, would be termed actual want. Some of them receive irregular remittances from relatives in the city, but many are dependent upon what they can glean from their sketchy cultivation of the soil. Cracked corn and peas form the basis of their diet.

Some experimentation was done in the effort to seek the proper relief measures for this widowed group, for many of them actually need assistance. The county gives little relief in any of its districts and its poor house has been closed because no one would go there. On St. Helena, six are on the poor list. They receive a total of $23.50 per month in amounts of three, four and five dollars apiece. Penn School is able to help some through its contributions from outside friends and through special island collections. Outsiders furnish garments for the sales house where they are passed on to the Islanders for a nominal sum or, in cases of actual need, for nothing. Occasionally school children are asked to bring in produce to be redistributed to the needy. These collections assemble contributions ranging from one potato up.

Our experimentation indicated, however, that what these unfortunates need as much as money and provisions is aid in cultivation of the land,—a little hired labor to plow or cultivate at a critical time; a little fertilizer to bring the crop along; perhaps some money for tuition so that one of the children may enter Penn School; perhaps medical attention to check malaria or purge hookworm. Each family is a study in itself.

This relatively stable family is an evolution. The slave passage wiped out African tribal marriage customs and replaced them with an artificially controlled monogamy on the plantation. Marriage customs varied from plantation to plantation. In the words of Carolina Bleach, "On our plantation dere was no marriaging. De man and de woman just stood up in front of Dr. Pope and he said, 'Do you want dis woman?' and 'Do you want dis man? All right, I will give you a house.'"

On some of the plantations marriage was more formal and a ceremony was performed by a minister. Some of the couples supplemented the informal approval of the master with a ceremony performed by the local "praise" leader. When freedom came many of the couples got married all over again.

Under slave management woman was supreme in the family. It was the wife who named and controlled the children. To her the weekly ration of provisions was issued and she was paid a bonus for any turned back. She looked after the garden patch and the chickens. She

THE HOME

ground the corn into meal and supervised the killing of hogs and chickens. To her cloth was issued to be made into clothing. She it was who sold chickens and eggs and bought extra delicacies from the store. The man was there for field work and service. Around the house he was an appendage, and the woman was very necessary for his comfort.

In fact, Miss Towne [2] records that one of the features of freedom most enjoyed by the men was freedom from the domestic domination of the women. Women have never needed emancipation on St. Helena.

From this plantation relationship the present family duties have evolved. In addition to performing the usual household duties, the woman is as important as the man in the farming operations. She tends the chickens and sometimes the other animals. After the man has plowed the garden she usually takes charge of that also. In the discussion of the successful farmers it was noted that in all of these cases the successful man had married an energetic woman and that in some cases widows were in the successful farmer group. Occasionally a couple divides their farm and the man and wife enjoy a keen rivalry in their husbandry.

Women do not hold official positions in the church, but are unofficially powerful in its organization and in the affairs of the praise house. The lodges or societies are usually separately organized for men and women.

Authority for making decisions in the family is usually divided, the woman governing the household and, to a large extent, the children, the man governing the farm and

[2] Holland, *Diary and Letters of Laura M. Towne.*

finances. Occasionally a strong personality will exert more influence than tradition has decreed for his or her sex.

Children are neither "don't-ed" to death nor allowed to "express themselves" by running roughshod over parents and neighbors. The rod is neither spared nor used to excess. The result is cheerful obedience to authority. They acquire a personality status in household and farm duties early. They begin by minor household duties, by picking up potatoes, picking cotton, or feeding the animals, —chores that are almost play for the farm child. From these they are gradually led into the heavier tasks of the farm and household. Boys of twelve and fourteen are usually taught to plow. "Manners" are emphasized. To be "no-manners" is disgraceful. To be unclean is "no-manners," likewise to fail to "pull de foot" and curtsey to one's elders, or to be nasty or lousy, or to violate any one of dozens of taboos.

Eighty per cent of those from six to sixteen are in school, and while they are kept out occasionally on account of bad weather or emergency duties on the farm, the "thing to do" with children is to give them schooling. They are not included in the wider community activities until adolescence when they become members of the church and begin to have thoughts of marriage.

Here we have none of the changes in the family which are beginning to attract so much attention, no innovations in the form of marriage, no new systems of rearing children, no new functions or powers for man or woman. In structure and function the family remains as it emerged from the plantation system.

THE HOME

The size of the family is still large, averaging four per household. It has previously been noted that several women have had over twenty-five children. In 1910 the Census counted the number of dead and living children of each mother. The total number averaged 6.75 per mother, and the number living averaged 3.8. Of the 1,100 mothers 184 had had over twelve children and seventy had had over fifteen children. In the 1928 enumeration the average number of living children was 2.8. The number is smaller now because migration has reduced the birthrate and increased the deaths of children moving to the city.

The family and the household are practically synonomous as there are only a negligible number of young couples living with their parents. The usual household includes a father, mother and their own children, or widow and her grandchildren or nephews. Quite a number of households have adopted members of the family, but practically none have lodgers.

The plantation is a larger extension of several families which have intermarried. It is a face-to-face neighborhood where relationship is complicated but well recognized. This closeness of neighborhood, the recognized family relationship, and the simple community organization, give the plantation a solidarity and unity of action which is remarkable. It is this community solidarity and close relationship which enables the church to exercise such efficient control over disputes.

When the lands were sold to the Negroes, cabins in "de street" or "de nigger house yaad," as the plantation quarters were formerly known, were moved to the center of the ten acre patches scattered all over the old plantation. Most of them show long standing marks of beautification. Old gnarled fig and pomegranate bushes, oleanders, great clumps of jonquils or phlox make the door-yard garden.

The majority of these first houses were one or two room cabins with stick and mud chimney. There were a scattering of larger houses embellished with bay windows and front porches. Under the constant pressure of Penn School for better homes the one-room houses have gradually disappeared and now only a few of this type are occupied by the older people.

The next type was the two-room house with a "jump up." The "jump up" corresponds, on a smaller scale, to the second story rooms placed under a bungalow roof. Sometimes it is approached by stair and sometimes by ladder. Here the children are given separate quarters.

The average house is now 3.3 rooms (including the "jump up") and the usual arrangement for a small family is one room for eating and living quarters, a room for the couple, and the "jump up" for the children. Often a small shed kitchen is added. In the larger families a bed is placed in the living and dining room, and in the more commodious houses the dining room and sitting room are separate. The front door usually opens into a small hallway which communicates with the other rooms.

With relatively small houses and large families there is of necessity some crowding. About 20 per cent of the households average more than two people per room. However, these include the families with five or more children, several of whom occupy common quarters. Overcrowding of this nature among the young folks is by no means serious. The general island averages are 3.3 rooms for four people.

The houses are all of frame, usually whitewashed. The doors and window shutters are painted blue and green. They are set up on palmetto post foundations and in many instances ceiled inside with tongue-and-groove boards. Brick chimneys have about replaced the stick and mud construction, and glass windows are in the majority of houses though only a few are screened. The walls are usually decorated with newspaper prints and a few cheap pictures.

Many of the earlier pieces of furniture were bought at the auction of plantation effects from which the older families have kept a few pieces of genuine worth. These are mingled with cheaper modern furniture and a few handmade pieces. A large number of the small houses are over-furnished in such items as tables and chairs, though the large family is often short on beds and bed clothing.

Cook stoves have replaced fireplace cooking in the majority of the houses and water is obtained by hand pumps from shallow driven wells. While there is not a well to every house, all of the houses are within convenient distance of water.

The constructive influence of Penn School on family life is five-fold. Its home demonstration agent improves diet and general homemaking activities. Its nurse looks after the health of the children and communicable diseases among the elders. It is interested in problems of morality. Its class rooms educate the children and its better home demonstrations are efforts to improve the house and its furnishings. The activities of the nurse, the home demonstration agent and the class room have been fully discussed in other chapters.

The relatively high illegitimacy rate was noted earlier in this chapter. In addition to the social pressure exerted by the church against this moral situation, Penn School reaches its pupils fairly successfully. One of the teachers has been to Hampton for a special course in sex education and hygiene, and has organized class room work adapted to the needs of the Island and influence is also exerted through the midwives' class and the community class.

The better homes demonstrations of the school have included constructive work in beautifying the house itself, the farm buildings, the premises, and the furnishings. These demonstrations have resulted in one of the most outstanding successes of the school's community program. They have received national recognition in the annual competitions between the communities of the United States in home improvement.

While the demonstration culminates in a better home week, the committee in charge of this activity operates the year round, planning and advising with those who wish to improve their living quarters. Other departments of the school, particularly the carpentry shop and the domestic science department, give continuous aid in home improvement. Refrigerators made in the shop and sanitary privies built by the boys are found scattered over the Island, and the domestic science department and community class are constantly quilting, planning gardens, and making draperies and bedclothes.

The young children are also successfully interested

THE HOME 217

through essays and contests. This is the production of a third grade boy on the subject:

"I am going to have a home, yes, a home. And what kind of home do you think I am going to have? A better home, yes, a better home, and I am going to see that I have my windows washed, walls papered and floors scrubbed and old tin cans buried, and my woodpile in the back yard, horse stable cleaned out and a lawn and plenty of flowers planted and a garden and a gig shelter.

"In order to have better homes we must follow rules, we must have everything clean about us. I am going to plant two trees in my front yard."

This work was begun by the school in 1922, when a teacher's cottage was used for demonstration, and the national third prize was won. The next year an average island house, in poor repair, was fixed up, white-washed and painted, furnished by the boys and girls, and exhibited after much publicity. This brought the second national prize. In 1924 the boys erected a model house out of second-hand lumber, keeping a careful budget of the cost. It was furnished by the carpentry shop and sewing department, and still serves as the domestic science practice house, winning the first school exhibit prize. To supplement this the pupils built small cardboard models of houses and these were carried from place to place on trucks for exhibit. This brought a special prize of $200. In succeeding years several "honorable mentions" have been awarded the island effort. In making one of these awards a national official wrote: "It is impressive to see once again the careful attention given to details, the large attendance, the wide-spread cooperation, the economy, simplicity, and wholesomeness which characterized your demonstration."

In this way humble aspirations are stimulated and pride of ownership is supplemented by pride in improvement. After three years' work, in spite of boll weevil conditions the committee found 988 improvements made. Improvements had been made in 171 individual homes and 26 new houses had been built.

Thus the family, the fundamental social unit of the Island, is helped in its diet by the home demonstration agent; in educating the children by the school; in sanitation and child care of the nurse; in sex morals by the school and the church; and in its housing and premises by the better homes campaign. The result is plainly visible to the casual observer in the disappearance of the one-room cabin, the increase in larger, neater houses, the low infant death rate, and the beautification of many places.

CHAPTER XI

PLAY

Down in the valley, O Lord!
Didn't go t' stay, O Lord!
My soul got happy, O Lord!
I stayed all day—

Little David, play on your harp, Hallelu'!

The art of "pleasuring yourself" on the Island is not highly developed. The days are filled with farm work for all but the young, and at night it is the custom to retire early. There are few opportunities for play, as such, except on holidays.

Religion and recreation are interwoven in many functions. Re-creation of the spirit and re-creation of the body are recognized as closely akin. The "shout" is a peculiar mingling of the spiritual and the physical relaxation. This ceremony occurs infrequently now. Formerly it was more common.

It begins when the prayer-meeting service in the praise house is over. After the benediction the benches are pushed against the walls, clearing the floor. The women form a ring and the men congregate in a corner. The men begin a spiritual with lively rhythm, clapping to emphasize the beats. The ring begins revolving, first slowly, then more energetically. The step is much like that which gained world fame as "The Charleston." Stamping is interspersed with shuffling. The feet are held close to the floor and dragged forward by a twist of the entire body. As the dance becomes more lively, elbows, hips, and shoulders are given greater play. This exercise requires energy, and there is constant dropping out and returning to the ring. This may go on for hours. Early missionaries tell of shouts lasting well toward daybreak, making sleep impossible within half a mile. To their pious sensibilities these "orgies" appeared to be remains of old idol worship.

There is a clear distinction between the shout and the devotional service, as shouting is never started until after the benediction. There is also a sharp line between shouting and dancing. The latter difference depends on the manipulation of the feet. To shuffle without crossing the feet is legitimate shouting; to "cross-um-foot" is a sin, and the older men among the singers have sharp eyes for foot crossing and call warnings to those whose exuberance leads the feet into danger.

This is a survival of the plantation gatherings. Slaves had little opportunity to assemble except for the plantation praise services. It was therefore natural that they should take advantage of this opportunity to add a recreational postscript to the evening.

The ceremonies and services of the church itself have their recreational values. This is especially true of the singing. On St. Helena singing is as much a mental release as golf is elsewhere. It is done in a whole-souled manner which precludes other mental activities. A funeral, a wedding, a baptizing, or even a regular Sunday service or praise house service becomes a social event, an oppor-

PLAY 221

tunity for self-expression and for the young people to meet and walk home together.

Ritual and ceremony are also attractive features of the lodge gatherings. The interminable "business meetings" and "turnouts" are fully and eagerly attended.

Although dancing is frowned on by the church, the few "ungodly" have occasional dances at private homes or lodge halls. These are accurately termed "rocks."

"Vine" and liquor play some part in leisure time stimulation, but little drunkenness is noticeable, and the magistrates' records indicate no serious abuse of the corn and berry crops.

In the summer there are ample opportunities for outdoor recreation for the young folks. The boys have marbles, tops, and baseball. Formerly baseball was very popular, most of the plantations having a team. This game, however, seems to have declined in popularity. Berrypicking and nut-gathering are also looked on as play as well as means of supplementing the larder.

The proximity of rivers and creeks adds greatly to the possibilities of outdoor play. There is not much swimming on account of "de critters" in the water, but a large number of people put in much time in fishing, some of them using more time in this way than is good for their farming program. The tidal rivers are alive with crabs and oysters, and in midsummer shrimp are plentiful. Shark, catfish, black fish, whiting, and sheepshead are caught with hand lines in quantities. A rarer but more prized catch is the great drumfish which sometimes attains the size of sixty pounds. When the sand flies begin to bite the natives know that it is time for drum to run, and the waters of the sound around the best "drops" are dotted with small sail boats and bateaux, whose occupants wait for hours for a single bite. When one of these great fish is brought in, a stew of the head is a rare treat. In the winter there is also torch fishing for trout. One man rows the flat-bottomed bateau while the other is poised in the prow with a torch to reveal the fish and a spear to bring him in.

Hunting is confined to rabbits and squirrels, since the rights over quail, deer, and duck have, since long before the Civil War, been reserved to white owners of near-by hunting preserves.

Picnics and excursions also enliven the summer program. The various plantations and Sunday School organizations have picnics during the summer. Excursions are usually made on chartered boats, most frequently to Savannah. At other times the Island is the objective of an excursion from the city. Then numbers of people who have moved away come back to renew home ties. The Fourth of July is an especially elaborate occasion. Excursions come in from both Charleston and Savannah, and the roads are crowded with second-hand cars of many makes all headed for home. Fish and lemonade booths are busy. There is speech-making, baseball, and dancing, as well as entertainments and family reunions in homes. There is a general home-coming of all ex-Islanders who can return, and a general turning-out of all Islanders who are at home. Money plays no large part in this fun. We have already referred to the experience of the store with one of these picnics when the cash register rang six hundred times for aggregate sales of only $37, an average of

COMMUNITY HOUSE

PLAY

about six cents per purchase. That is the extent of high-flying.

Much of the play of the young people has been developed by Penn School. The early missionaries commented especially on the absence of games among the children, and there is still much aimless standing around. This situation has, however, been somewhat remedied by the teaching of games at the school and training the public school teachers to direct play.

The apparatus of the school is much in demand all during the day and even into the early evening, and the dancing and marching games learned at recess are often continued at home.

The school has also developed some adult amusements. Periodical community sings and picture shows are enjoyed. A community class for the older women meets once a week for sewing and singing. In addition, pageantry is connected with the farmer's fair, the school finals, better homes week, and other public occasions.

These are wholesome ranges of leisure time activities, especially since the roads make gathering difficult in the winter and the work on the farm occupies much of the time of men, women and children during the summer, leaving them too fatigued at night for recreation away from home. Within the home music is the chief diversion. Some families have victrolas and a few have organs or other instruments. For the most part, however, the music is vocal. There are few banjos, and in the early days of evangelism the missionaries reported the silencing of many violins which have remained silent.

There are practically no books and magazines in the

home. The library in the community house is well patronized. Through this library and the county library boxes sent out to the public schools there was a circulation of over twelve hundred books in 1928-29.

Between work and worship the adults have little time to play, but through the constant use of song and rhythm the spirit of play has been woven into many phases of work and worship.

CHAPTER XII

RELIGION

Yes, eb'ry time I feels de sperit
Movin' in muh heart
I will pray.

Preacher, you better preach so,
So Jesus can use you,
Oh, you better preach so,
So Jesus can use you
At any time, any time, any time.

In the prayers and songs the emotional experience of the Islanders, which centers around worship, takes on a vividness and depth which is hardly to be entered into by a member of another race. Their reality cannot be doubted by one who observes the earnestness of expression, the postures, the nodding, the exclamations.

Often men pray until their voices break and the sweat pours from their faces. When this point is reached the emotions of the audience are also in full sway and they begin softly to sing a spiritual. Soon the song blends with the prayer. As the voices of the congregation swell louder than that of the supplicant, the prayer fades out and the song goes on.

The very manner in which religious experience enters the life of a young person is foreign to present American church practices. It reaches back to the beginnings of Protestant worship when candidates for membership were instructed by "class leaders" and tested by dreams and visions. This process, in the Sea Islands, is termed "seeking" and usually begins, with adolescence, around the age of 13 or 14. The custom is also reminiscent of the African initiation ceremonies in which the young retire into the bush for a period of testing and are then instructed in the business of life by the older members of the tribe.

Instead of beginning religious experience under the emotional sway of a revival or of an eloquent sermon, the seeker begins with a dream or vision, sometimes with conscious effort to induce a dream or vision. Any unusual dream at this period may be interpreted as the beginning of the search for salvation. After the first dream the candidate begins to fast and pray in the woods at night. Soon an older member of the community is indicated in a dream or vision as the "teacher." If the "teacher" has had a dream or vision which may be interpreted to have some point in common, the older person and the seeker assume the teacher-pupil relationship. One woman said that she had dreamed of a silver leaf and a silver needle and soon a seeker came to her who had dreamed of a silver pot, so they knew she was indicated as his teacher.

One seeker dreamed that she was walking out Eddings Point Road with a candle and found a baby in the road. After attending to the baby she walked on and found it again on returning. This signified the finding of her soul. Then she dreamed of a dish of beans and the name of her teacher. We are somewhat in the dark as to the significance of the beans unless she had been fasting. There were further prayers at night in the woods, and more dreams which were recounted to the teacher and interpreted. Finally after prayer in the woods, lasting almost through the night, a voice just before daybreak said: "Your sins are forgiven and your soul set free." She awoke feeling happy and singing a spiritual. Her teacher knew she was "through."

After this period of seeking the candidate is instructed in church lore and doctrine by the teacher and is examined, first by the praise house committee, and then by the deacons of the church. From two weeks to three months are required for seeking. Some teachers become careless and let their seeker get lost. Some seekers get into bad company during the trial or show bad traits and are turned down.

It is evident from the vividness of memory concerning the details of these episodes that conversion is a psychological experience which is very real to the seekers and that after passing through this experience they feel themselves to be, and doubtless are, different personalities.

When the deacons have examined the candidates and decided that the proper period of seeking has been passed, they are baptized in the good old-fashioned way in the tidal creek. Baptizings are held every quarter when there are candidates and the whole church turns out. Before baptizing the candidates are careful to keep their minds free from frivolity. For several weeks they do not attend parties or go out much.

Weddings, while presided over by the preacher and always sanctioned by the church, are not held in the church but in the residence of the bride.

Funerals are also state occasions, well attended. A formal "sitting up" of several days usually precedes the funeral. The lengths to which the Islanders will go to see that the "sitting up" is properly solemnized is indicated by the fact that bodies are sometimes kept unembalmed until they have to be "buried shallow" to await the scheduled funeral time.

A funeral of a prominent citizen was attended. The man died on the preceding Saturday, but his body had been embalmed. The weather was clear and the services were held in the front yard of the man's home. Some three hundred people were present. Very few of these remained close to the center of things throughout the service. There was much going back and forth, talking, laughing, starting cars, and other activity. It was clear that the funeral was a great social event. After two or three hymns and four or five addresses by ministers and other prominent people, the coffin was carried to the hearse. There had been no sign of grief until the pall bearers lifted the coffin. Then there arose considerable wailing from the porch where the relatives had been sitting. One young woman, sister of the deceased, ran toward the hearse in a hysterical fashion and had to be taken in charge by a man.

Two Negro women had accompanied us and they were eager to go to the cemetery also. The procession was slow in getting off, so we drove on ahead for about a mile. Then one of the women said we had better stop and wait. She was not sure which way they would turn. If the man's wife gets control of the body they will bury it at one place, but if the sister gets the body they will bury it at another. We waited until the procession came along. It seems that the sister won in this family squabble, and we had only three miles to go. If the wife had won the distance would have been greater. The cemetery was a typical island graveyard. It was such a tangle of trash and brush that it was very difficult for more than a dozen people to get close enough to the grave to see. The earth mounds were covered with household articles and dishes. It is the custom to place on top of the grave those articles most cherished by the departed. Here repose antique dishes, lamps, alarm clocks, and a heterogeny of other small articles.

When we arrived the grave was not quite finished, but it was ready in a few minutes. The coffin was placed on the automatic lowering apparatus and while someone played *Nearer, My God, to Thee* on a small organ which had been brought to the graveyard, the coffin was allowed to drop slowly into the grave. This was a signal for loud mourning. The relatives had been very calm but now they rushed to the side of the grave and began to "take on." The man's wife was rather calm in her grief, but the sister grew hysterical again and had to be supported by a man. As the grave was being filled, the relatives withdrew to the outer edge of the trees where their cries could be heard, but after a few moments the sounds died away. There was a brief ceremony around the grave by one of the lodges. Then a hymn was lined while the grave was being filled. The leader did not have his hymn book. When he reached the limit of his memory he had to stop. One man then led a spiritual, *Don't Do Dat*, which was somewhat out of place, since he was at the time shoveling dirt into the grave as fast as he could. It was beginning to drizzle rain, and the services were cut short. We understood that there would have been quite a bit of singing at the graveside if the weather had been good. But the grave was hurriedly covered and oak sticks were thrust in as head and foot boards, a benediction was said and all was over.

Another ceremony which partakes of the religious nature is the house blessing, a simple service to dedicate the new house. When the dwelling is ready for occupancy the neighborhood members of the praise house gather for a few simple, earnest prayers and rhythmic spirituals.

The lodges and societies also hold their principal annual "turn out" in connection with the church. For the larger organizations a Sunday service is set aside. The members come with banners, sashes, and embroidered aprons, and the minister gives them a special sermon. They remember their dead and honor their living. At this service the usual prayers and songs are added to the marching and ritualistic hand clapping of the order.

Thus the church prescribes all of the principal ceremonies of the Islanders—weddings, funerals, house blessings, and lodge celebrations. The only occasions which are without benefit of the clergy are the school "finals" and the occasional picnics. Prayer is often offered at these functions.

In all these ceremonies and in the regular Sunday service there is a simple dignity and restraint not usually conveyed in literary accounts of Negro worship. Probably the levity of the authors arises from the occasional grotesquerie of the words used and the interjections of the congregation. If, however, the white listener can penetrate beyond the word itself to the meaning which it is intended to convey and the feeling it implies, a more dignified impression is carried away.

At the Sunday service the attendance is large. Over the twisting island roads they come for miles, afoot, in buggies, carts and cars. Everyone, no matter how poor, wears a Sunday suit or dress. Most of these have been carefully preserved for several years, but they are conspicuously sober and neat.

The buildings are above the average of rural churches—more like the smaller city structures. The audience divides by sex, with the deacons and older members seated on benches at the front and running at right angles to the others. The choir is in a balcony at the rear of the audience and facing the minister.

Old hymns and spirituals are sung, hymns predominating. None of the congregation have hymn books, so the hymn is announced: "Number 245 Common Meter," or "Number 300 Long Meter." The leader lines out a verse and the congregation sings it, then he lines out another.

The sermons which we heard were expository and not so fervent as usually heard in the middle class Negro church. Reverend D. C. Washington, the dean of the island ministers, speaks deliberately and, as he is educated, he speaks practically without dialect. There are, however, in his discourse, periods of emotional fervency when the congregation joins in with exclamations of "Do, Jesus" and "Yes, Lord."

But let us attend church. The service begins late, although a large crowd has been gathering in the church yard. We are ushered to a pew in the second row. The benches are in good repair and have been treated with a stain in a ziz-zag fashion which gives them an appearance of having been carved. The walls above the lower wood panel are of smooth white plaster, cracked and stained with water in many places. To the right and left of the pulpit there are two or three rows of benches set at right angles to the other benches. These are occupied by the older men. To the right of the pulpit a door opens into a rear room, and during the service it is used quite frequently. The bread and wine for communion are being prepared in this room. One deacon after another gets up and goes into the room.

Service opens with a spiritual, *No Harm*. The leader sings very loudly with perfect rhythm, and does not hesitate to swing his body and pat his hands. He stands just in front of the rostrum. His son sits in the gallery leading the choir. At times it looks as if father and son are trying to see who can sing the louder. After the spiritual comes the prayer, rhythmic, sing-song, and with rising cadences and plenty of help from the "Amen corner." As the prayer reaches a climax, someone softly starts a spiritual. As others join, the song rises in volume, and for a minute or two song and prayer rise together. The song ascends and the prayer is heard no longer. Then there are a few words by the regular pastor, a hymn lined by the leader and sung in lugubrious cadence, another prayer, and the scripture reading, and another slow hymn. Next comes the sermon on Citizenship. It is an exposition of the rights and duties of citizens, couched, for the most part, in restrained language. However, the minister grows fervent at times and almost lapses into the old style of preaching.

RELIGION

At these points some of the pious brethren call out, "Step on the gas," "Push, man, push," etc. The sermon is full of sound and homely advice, but it is evident that the burden of the message has to do with Prohibition. There have recently been some cases of public drinking.

After the sermon there is another prayer, and some words about "our white wisitors."

Collection is taken, under the sway of the spiritual, *Death So Hard on Me.* This is the most interesting part of the service. The leader waves his arms and shuffles around in a very spry way. The members file forward to deposit their money on the table where two deacons sit to count it. Some of the marchers shuffle and sway to the music. The leader pats them on the back or touches their arms, so that the procession looks somewhat like a country dance. One or two old women sway in their seats and finally stand up and shuffle as if they are about to break into a "shout." The members give as much as they can afford. It is promptly counted, and as the last coin rings on the table one of the counters rises and announces thanks for the $21.12.

After the collection there were some announcements as to communion service which was to follow, another hymn and finally the benediction. Those who stayed for communion probably remained until about four o'clock.

The communion service is held quarterly and is much more of a function than the regular service. The dates are arranged so that the quarterly services of different churches fall on different dates, and there is much visiting from one church to another on these Sundays. The best singers of the visiting choirs are merged with the regular choir and spirited music is the result.

The organization is overwhelmingly Baptist. In fact, the one small Methodist church, composed of the descendants of refugee families which came in during the Civil War, has practically ceased to operate. There are six Baptist churches on St. Helena proper, one on Coosaw Island, and two on Ladies Island.

By adhering to the Baptist creed, the Islanders have followed the example of the majority of their former masters and have demonstrated their preference for the form of worship which allows them the maximum of self-government and self-expression. The planters were predominantly Baptist, with a minority of Episcopalians. While the Episcopal diocese conducted some missionary activity among the slaves, there is no evidence that their efforts bore fruit in any appreciable number of converts. Dr. Fuller, a Baptist minister who owned land on St. Helena, and other earlier Baptist missionaries who made their rounds of the plantations numbered their converts by the hundreds.

It is Dr. Fuller and a Mr. Hardy who are quaintly remembered in St. Helena's version of *Roll, Jordan, Roll:*

> "Dr. Fuller sittin' on de tree ob life
> For to yeddy, ol' Jerdan, roll,
> Roll, Jerdan, roll, Jerdan,
> Roll, Jerdan, roll.

> "Mr. Hardy sittin' on de tree ob life," etc.

Since this was an area where the masters did not remain the year round, there was practically no opportunity for the slaves to attend with the masters as they did in some other Southern sections. Services in the white churches were held only during a few winter months when the owners were in residence, and then not every Sunday. The small size of the galleries of the white churches indicate that, even during the period when services were held, only a handful of Negroes could have been accommodated in the gallery—probably only the coachmen and footmen who brought the owners.

Services for slaves were held once or twice a month by missionaries who came over from the mainland and made the plantation rounds, and in between these visits the praise houses assembled the plantation folk two or three times a week for services conducted by the praise leader.

The present distribution of the six Baptist churches on St. Helena proper has resulted from a series of splits caused mostly by disputes over the selection of ministers. The original Brick Church, which was taken over from the white people after the Civil War, now has Ebenezer, just across the tidal creek. About five miles farther on another off-shoot of Brick Church has split again and there is another pair of churches located just across the road from each other. Two other churches are located near each other on the south end of the Island about six miles from Brick Church.

This gives the Islanders a church for each 600 people—not an excessive number when compared to rural areas in general. However, Ebenezer enrolls well over a thousand members, and Brick Church is above the average in size. The others are rather small.

These six churches support only two resident pastors

and one of these supplements his income by farming and odd jobs. The other ministerial services are supplied by pastors from the mainland who share their time between a St. Helena pastorate and one or two churches elsewhere.

The fiscal and temporal affairs of the church are cared for by the regulation board of deacons who are very proud of their office and attentive to their duties.

By far the most unique feature of the religious organization is the survival to the present time of the ante-bellum "Praise House," a purely plantation institution which has become a branch of the church.

After the slave laws discouraged the gathering of slaves away from their own plantation, masters allowed their people to worship in plantation groups, usually at the house of one of the older people, sometimes in a special praise house. The "leaders" of these plantation groups were persons of considerable authority in spiritual matters. They have been referred to as the lineal descendant of the African medicine man, and they were the fore-runners of the present Negro ministers. They presided over meetings, gave spiritual advice, and in some cases officiated at weddings and funerals.

With the breakdown of ante-bellum plantations and the shifting of the freed population, praise houses disappeared from most sections to be supplanted by churches. In the Sea Islands churches were organized but were merely superimposed upon the praise house system, and on St. Helena the praise house remains the local, face-to-face unit of worship. Here services are held on three nights in the week, while churches hold services only on Sunday.

As we approach one of these houses to attend a regular

evening meeting, the lamp-light shines through the crevices and board shutters. There is no doubt as to the antiquity of the building, for it nestles beneath a great oak halfhidden by a screen of cassina bushes such as only time can erect. It is built of log framing, with rough clapboards on the sides and roofed with hand-split shingles. Inside the oil lamp yellows the small pine pulpit of the leader, but leaves the faces of the audience almost in the dark. The floor is uneven and the hand-made benches have no backs.

Only a few are seated at first, but as they sing the others soon gather until there are ten or twelve young people and ten or twelve of their elders, all neighbors from the surrounding plantation. There is the usual quota of spirituals, of slow hymns lined out by the leader and intoned by the audience, several earnest prayers, and the reading of a passage of scripture. The reading is expounded in homely phrase, paraphrased in the local dialect.

Sometimes, more rarely than in the past, there is a "shout" after the benediction. This is not a part of the service and partakes in spirit more of the recreational flavor. It has been described more fully, therefore, in the section on recreation.

There are from one to four praise houses on each plantation. As the churches have split, praise houses have also divided. Usually members of the praise house are members of the same church. Each plantation within the radius of influence of the two larger churches has two praise houses, one for each church. Sometimes subdivisions have added more.

Besides regular tri-weekly devotions, special "praise" is held on special occasions—a good harvest, or the recovery of a good neighbor. It is customary to hold praise at the houses of people who are very sick. After a whole night of singing and praying the invalid has been known to arise the next day completely cured.

The praise house is essentially a community institution. Here there is a face-to-face gathering of neighbors for the purpose of worship and the promotion of community solidarity. It is the unit on which the church is built. It is the center for spreading news. Does the school and the demonstration agent desire to warn of the approach of the boll weevil? The rounds of the praise houses are made. Should the people be warned that the last date for payment of taxes is approaching? News is sent to the praise leaders. Here the community in simplest form initiates its business and promotes law and order.

Undoubtedly it is this tight religious organization which keeps crime at a minimum in the township. Its people know of no crime wave, as there is little serious crime. They settle most cases through the church and praise house. This trait of the community will doubtless surprise those who consider that the Negro has inherent criminal tendencies.

The township magistrates' records reveal that, for a period of twenty years, the number of cases sent up to the circuit court averaged only two per year. In this respect the Island apparently does not differ materially from other rural communities of the section. The records of the magistrate of Sheldon, a mainland township, reveal an even smaller number of cases "bound over" to the higher court.

The church also takes a hand in disputes on the mainland.

Occasionally there is a scuffle and fight, in the heat of an argument, but seldom is there any trouble after the disputants have cooled off. More rarely there is a larceny prosecution growing out of misappropriation of animals or firewood, but there are no locks on the doors of island houses.

Other factors there are in the control of crime, but the machinery of the church is dominant. The other influences are: home ownership, with no sharp contrasts in economic and social status; absence of any considerable number of white people and consequent freedom from race friction and irritation; Penn School, actively interested for over sixty years in the promotion of morality and orderliness; the lodges and societies which, like the churches, have committees for settling disputes.

The church and praise house have a definite organization for settling disputes and thereby preventing crimes of violence. When a dispute arises among them, it is referred to one of two committees appointed for that purpose. If these are unable to compose the difference, the matter goes to the church council which is made up of a leader and a deacon from each praise house. Finally, the matter may be debated before the membership of the church as a whole.

The secular law is known as the "unjust law," and rather than resort to this law the injured man reports to the praise house committee. If he resorts to the courts first, he is automatically adjudged to be in the wrong, and he himself is likely to be arraigned before the church.

Restitution is the keynote of the decisions of these councils. The practical value to the injured man of receiving restitution, rather than merely seeing his opponent fined or punished by a county court, doubtless appeals strongly for the system.

Local magistrates wisely recognize this extra-legal machinery and encourage the people to compose their differences outside of court. When one of these magistrates caught a woman taking cloth from his own store he reported her to the Woman's Labor Union where she was humiliated by suspension and a fine of five dollars. The records of the magistrates indicate the reliance on this system to supplement their courts. The books of one court for a five-year period show four cases of assault and battery and seven cases of larceny disposed of by compromise.

Several cases of trespass are marked "dismissed on payment of damage to prosecutor." One entry for "assault and battery of a high and aggravated nature, with intent to kill," is marked "case dropped by prosecution, see letter in my possession." We accompanied the magistrate one day as he went out, without a fee, to settle a dispute which had not officially come before him. One man had originally owned a cow and left her with another who had cared for her a number of years. The latter "had bought de rope and paid de tax." When the original owner returned, bossy's status was warmly contested. The magistrate selected a community leader to accompany him and spent several hours of his time solemnly hearing the argument and rendering a compromise decision which seemed perfectly satisfactory.

By ironing out disputes in their initial stage, crimes of

BAPTIZING

RELIGION

violence are not only prevented, but civil suits are also almost completely avoided.

The averages of a twenty-year period indicate that the township magistrate's court has annually about thirty-five cases, of which twenty-eight are found guilty. There is no way of telling from the records which of these are outsiders offending in the township and which are residents. A check of a recent year, however, indicated that about half the total and nearly all the serious charges were against non-residents.

Of the twenty-eight found guilty, four are given suspended sentence or merely put under a bond to keep the peace, sixteen are fined, two sent to the higher court, two jailed, and four given miscellaneous penalties. These latter include the cases which are settled by the church machinery after getting into court, usually on the basis of restitution. The fines are rarely more than $10 except for the rare cases of carrying concealed weapons or violation of the game laws. Imprisonment is usually for thirty days.

The twenty-eight annual convictions divide as follows: eight for assault and battery, eight miscellaneous minor offenses, four disorderly conduct, four breach of peace, three larceny or burglary, one carrying concealed weapons. Three-fourths are for emotional outbursts which result in a fight or abuse too suddenly for the church machinery to intervene.

The remarkable feature of the power of the community machinery is the lack of official force behind it. Community pressure is the only backing it has. Expulsion from the community institutions and ostracism are the only ultimate penalties which can be inflicted for non-conformity. Some non-conformists are eventually allowed to go before the criminal court, but the majority fall in line.

It will be interesting to learn just how far the bridge and the greater mobility of population will change this situation. There are already some indications of change in the slight increase in violence among the migrants who return and visitors from the mainland. In the present simple community, however, the Islanders seem able to handle anti-social tendencies adequately by social pressure through their own institutions.

This phase of community development must be credited entirely to the Negroes themselves. They did get their early church organization from white example, but they have preserved the local unit and the power of the church in the community through their own efforts. By doing this they have evolved a power for the church in community affairs which can hardly be matched in any other neighborhoods in this country.

CHAPTER XIII

THE WORTH OF THE EXPERIMENT

I've got a home in the rock,
Don't you see?
I've got a home in the rock,
Don't you see?
Just between the earth and sky
Where my poor Jesus bled and die,
I've got a home in the rock,
Don't you see?

Two generations have been reared and the third is coming up since Pierce wrote to President Lincoln that the people of the Sea Islands had in them great possibilities of improvement provided wise measures were adopted to "elevate them and prepare them to be self-supporting citizens." Enough time has elapsed to begin to see the results of the forces which have operated.

Social precedents have counted for little in shaping the St. Helena community. Experiment has prevailed. Here precedents have been made rather than followed. Antebellum planters experimented with larger slaveholdings than others, and with new agricultural methods. The reconstruction government experimented in fostering Negro land ownership, and in sending teachers and missionaries to the freedmen. Penn School is still experimenting in developing industrial and agricultural education and adapting its program to the stimulation of the activities of the community.

On this Island was the first community of Negro landowners, the first Southern Negro school, the first agricultural cooperative in South Carolina, one of the first Negro community nurses, and here pioneering work has been done in adapting the work of farm and home demonstration agents to the needs of Negro farmers.

At the beginning of these experiments the working material was none too promising. It consisted of several thousand pure-blooded Negroes, demoralized by war, and lacking both in training for independent farming, and in experience with community affairs. They had a knowledge of the cultivation of cotton and corn and an acquaintanceship with hard work. Isolation had preserved the strength of tradition so that many of the affairs of life were governed by the superstitions of Africa. Tradition also bequeathed them a wealth of song and story to enrich their lives. Of these people, one of the reconstruction agents wrote: "We found them a herd of suspicious savages."

If progress can be made with such a group, then similar methods may be relied upon to show even greater results when applied to people who have had more advantages. Thus the experiment on St. Helena throws light upon the question as to what can be accomplished with a group of pure-blooded, isolated Negroes, when they are given the stimulus of intelligent paternalism.

In judging whether or not the experience on St. Helena is applicable to other Negro communities, it is well to note the points of similarity and of difference between the Island and other Southern areas. Originally the sea island

THE WORTH OF THE EXPERIMENT 245

Negroes were the same mixture of many African tribes. Our investigation did not support the theory that the coast was peopled by a special breed. They went through substantially the same slave experiences except that the contacts were more limited because they were in larger slave groups and were more isolated. After emancipation they, like others in the South, became cotton farmers.

The principal differences between the Island and other Southern areas have been the relative isolation, the ownership of land by the Negroes, and the operation of the constructive influence of Penn School. The strength of tradition in an isolated area has made constructive work more difficult, but the ownership of land and the independence of owners have made it easier. The organization and outlook on life of a community of landowners is radically different from that of Negro tenants occupying the lands of white owners. The tenant is dependent upon his landlord for land, food, clothes, and operating credit. The owner is independent. He plants what he pleases and is stimulated by pride of ownership. He "stays put," while half the tenants move every year or two to a different farm. It could not be expected, therefore, that a Penn School, put to work in a tenant area, could accomplish as much as it has done on St. Helena. Adaptations to suit tenant conditions would be necessary, but the fundamental experiences of this institution in improving health, diet, education, and morals, are applicable to other Negro rural communities.

Probably the most radically experimental step in the development of the community was the action of the National Government in selling the lands of the former masters to the newly liberated Negroes. Though the ex-slaves were inexperienced and ill-prepared for this transition, little aid was given to them in meeting their problems as the National Government soon withdrew and left them to live off their newly acquired holdings as best they could.

Under the circumstances the local county and state governments could not have been expected to contribute materially to the growth of the community. The whole area was so impoverished by war, that government expenditures even for white institutions were limited. In addition the attitudes created by war and by reconstruction were such that the feeling of Southern officials and taxpayers was inimical to measures which would extend government paternalism to the freedmen. A prominent citizen of Beaufort summed up the situation by saying that "the Yankees took the land from the Southern owners for taxes, and turned it over to the Negroes, and the Southerners would, therefore, be justified by taking it back by the same process." At present this attitude bears fruit in the taxation of the township for the benefit of the institutions of the other parts of the county,—the payment into the county treasury, by the Islanders, of more money than they receive back in their meagre appropriations for roads and public schools.

Because the National Government withdrew, and the local governments were uninterested in fostering the experiment of building a Negro landowning community, this development was left to the devices of the Negroes themselves, with such paternalistic aid as private philanthropy might provide. And it would seem that if a situation ever

THE WORTH OF THE EXPERIMENT 247

justified paternalism, the situation in which the freedmen found themselves, through no act of their own, was one which called for such a policy both on the part of the government and of private philanthropic organizations.

Penn School has been the agency through which private philanthropy functioned in the community. It has planned the activities and secured the funds for carrying them on. The constructive forces have been largely set in motion and directed by this institution. It has brought education and training in morality and industry. For the adults, it has made available the services of the nurse, the home demonstration agent, the farm demonstration agent, recreational facilities, and modern ideas on many lines. It has made the Island an outstanding example of the possibilities of these forces in rural community development. One can hardly fail to speculate on the probable improvement in the Southern racial situation if the whole area had been dotted with Penn Schools.

The demonstration of the improvability of health, family welfare, economic activity, and religion,—the fundamentals of life,—has been so convincing that other Southern counties could well afford to assume as government functions some of the semi-private activities of Penn School. Public health nursing, farm demonstration, home demonstration, and the teaching of agriculture, have all come to be recognized as legitimate government activities in rural districts. The problem of the South is to discover the people and develop the means to make these functions as effective for Negroes as for white people; and as effective for both races in all areas as they are on the Island.

Nor is the value of the St. Helena experiment confined to the United States. In Asia, Africa, and the Near East, civilized governments are confronted with the problems of dealing with masses of backward people. These people derive their incomes from agriculture, and their satisfactions from rural life. Here the most efficient form which paternalism can assume is the development of the masses in the fundamental activities of life. This comes through the sponsorship and finance of organizations capable of stimulating these essential functions. In this task government and private philanthropy have a divided responsibility.

If missionary activity means the fuller development of the capabilities of a backward people, then the social objectives of the missionaries and of the paternalistic mandate and colonial governments are the same. Striking examples of successful methods and policies are to be found for both groups in this experiment of the development of the St. Helena community.

In balancing the books on this experiment, a review of the preceding pages indicates many facts creditable to the community as a going concern and a few phases of life in which the Islanders have not adapted themselves to American standards.

The population increases steadily by excess of births over deaths. There are more people on the Island than there were in slavery. Recent migration has taken some of the younger people to the city, but there is comparatively little movement of whole families except when one parent dies and the other members drift off. At that, the

THE WORTH OF THE EXPERIMENT 249

loss from St. Helena has not been so great as that from most of the cotton counties of the rural South. After the Islanders reach the city, a good proportion of them attain the average standards of city Negroes, and their early training keeps them from difficulty with the law.

In health, the showing of St. Helena was most favorable. From a community with no health facilities, excellent public health work has developed. The fragments of evidence extant indicate that this area was most unhealthy before the Civil War. White people would only live there in the winter and slave death rates were high. Now the island death rate has been reduced to the normal rate of other Negro communities. A full-time nurse and doctor serve the people. Superstition and reliance upon patent medicines have been rapidly replaced by modern medical practises. Tuberculosis is well controlled, and confined to cases brought back from the city. Pneumonia is rare. Typhoid is negligible. There is little reliable evidence as to the prevalence of venereal diseases, but the indications are that these, like tuberculosis, are brought in from the city. The only other contagious or infectious disease which accounts for an appreciable number of deaths is malaria, and this is held below the average of the sea coast area. The infant mortality rate is so low as to be listed as an outstanding achievement. Certainly in health matters, a most fundamental phase of life, the Islanders have adopted the best American standards.

A yeoman standard of living, not entirely dependent upon money economy, has developed. The estimated average money income of $420 on the Island includes much food produced at home and the use of an owned house, both of which would cost more dearly in the city. For this reason the island income is equivalent to about $20 per week in the city. The bulk of the Islanders have a good house, good diet, but few clothes and no luxuries. Agriculture, the principal method of breadwinning, has been developed to a higher plane than that of tenant farming, where the whole attention of the farmer is focussed on cotton. The island farmers have always diversified their crops more and bred more animals. Since the advent of the boll weevil, the agricultural department of Penn School and the farm demonstration agent have greatly increased this diversification. There is much room for improvement in the breeding of animals through the selection of better stock and provision of better pastures. Crop yields could be increased through the use of more fertilizer. While agriculture is in serious straits owing to the general unfavorable economic conditions and to the boll weevil, many of the Island farmers manage to feed themselves and make a little cash while almost 10 per cent feed themselves well and average around $600 per year.

The Islanders take advantage of their educational opportunities. An exceptionally large proportion of the older people have been to school for a short time and four-fifths of the children from six to sixteen are enrolled in school. The public schools are poorly financed but improving. In Penn School the Island has an industrial and agricultural school unique in its community outlook and thorough in its instruction. Throughout the range of island life, in health, in agriculture, in family life and housing, and in morals, the influence of Penn School is felt.

The normal family—a man, wife, and children—is the

fundamental social organization. The head of the family is the patriarch and the authority. Through the efforts of Penn School and its better homes demonstration the homes have been greatly improved. The one-room cabin has almost disappeared and the mode is the story and a half house with a sprinkling of two-story dwellings. Better-homes Week is an island festival. Stimulated by well-selected examples, hundreds of families have brightened their dwelling with paint, added a porch or rooms, or made repairs. The work of the home demonstration agent in improving diet and home management is also influential in family life. Through her efforts the canning clubs now put up over five thousand cans and jars of vegetables and fruits annually.

The religious organization is strong. The church is much more of a factor in the control of the sea island communities than in the average modern community. Not only is it the place of worship, and to some extent of recreation, but through its peculiar organization of branch "praise houses," it also settles the disputes of the community. This active control by church committees has held crime at a minimum.

There are three principal points at which the Islanders have not adapted to American standards:

Most fundamental is a rather easy-going attitude toward life, held by the great majority,—a contentment with less than would satisfy the average American family. This is a survival of the standards of the slave street where less than twenty dollars a year sufficed to feed and clothe a slave. That such satisfaction is not universal is indicated by the drift of many young people to the city, but for the majority who remain, life is an Oriental pursuit of a calm, unhurried destiny, rather than a drive under the spur of ambition. At this point, however, it must be remembered that the Island standards are *sui generis* and the inhabitants have not known other standards except by hearsay. Their way of living at least enables them to live longer, if not so luxuriously.

Associated with this relative lack of ambition is the failure of most of the families to accumulate that surplus which is essential to progress. The little surplus which the boll weevil left was swept away recently in a Beaufort bank failure, and at present the Island savings, for the most part, are represented by a few small deposits in the safe of the local merchant. In this respect, however, St. Helena is little different from the balance of the communities of small-scale cotton and tobacco farmers. The culture of these crops does not bring wealth. Only the most ambitious and energetic of these farmers, whether white or black, have much to show for a life of toil beyond the subsistence of their families and the ownership of land. The Islanders, like other black belt farmers, have been bound to a system in which the lean years consumed most of the surplus of the fat, and the purchase of a few comforts dissipated the balance.

The third principal aberration from American standards is the relative laxity of sex morals, evidenced by the high illegitimacy rate and the ease with which migration disrupts the family, leaving the women to bear the brunt of the job of rearing the children. It was pointed out, however, that about 60 per cent of the families were headed

THE WORTH OF THE EXPERIMENT 253

by couples living together as other American couples, and 35 per cent by widows or widowers who had once been married. Many of the parents of illegitimate children marry after the birth of the first child so that in this respect the sex code is similar to that of other peasant communities.

In short, the achievement on St. Helena has been an orderly community, a healthy community, one which is fairly stable, but in which breadwinning is difficult. A child born there has excellent chances for intelligent mothering, survival of children's diseases, healthy, outdoor play, good schooling, and absence from exposure to the vicious elements of society. If he has capabilities as a farmer he grows up to have his own land, his own home, and his own family. He makes a competence but not a fortune.

The inner workings of the adult community are probably most visible at the farmer's fair. The crowd begins to drift in to Penn School for this function early, many leaving home at "dayclean." One brings a coop of turkeys, another a pig. The women come with samples of canned goods, flowers, and handwork, the men with peanuts, potatoes, sugar cane, and corn. Each brings the best fruits of a year's work to be compared with the best fruits of others.

Even at the fair the influence of the church is felt, as the preacher opens and closes the event. The occasion is enlivened by the singing of spirituals. The song leader who is called upon does not lead unless the spirit is with him, but, fortunately, today the spirit is so. He mounts the platform, closes his eyes, spreads his arms and literally draws melody from the audience.

> "If you want to get to heaven
> I'll tell you how.
> Jus' wrap yo' hands
> Around dat plow."

The morning session is "experience." Successful farmers tell how "they did it," and the audience listens breathlessly and cross-questions keenly. The afternoon is given to the inspection of exhibits, awarding of prizes and a barbecue at which a whole cow is consumed.

At this fair, the mainsprings of life are discussed and exhibited,—the field crops, the animals, the food products, and the handwork. Blue and red ribbons are taken home pridefully to be hung in a prominent place.

In the early dusk the crowd disperses to travel homeward over the rutted, winding roads, each couple discussing the means of winning an award of merit at the next fair, and planning the disposal of the money it may bring. The decision may fall upon an added room in the home, the tuition and expenses of sending a boy off to school, or it may mean increased participation in the church and other community activities.

As the ox-carts creak and the buggy wheels swish through the sand, a voice may be heard rolling over the marshes:

> "Lawd, I wish I had an eagle's wings.
> Lawd, I wish I had an eagle's wings.
> O Lawd, wish I— O Lawd, wish I,
> O Lawd, wish I had an eagle's wings.

ANTE-BELLUM EPISCOPAL CHURCH

AN ISLAND GRAVE
The clock is a genuine antique with embossed silver pendulum

"I would fly all de way to Paradise.
I would fly all de way to Paradise.
O Lawd, fly all— O Lawd, fly all—
O Lawd, fly all de way to Paradise."

HOW WE GOT ACQUAINTED

The method of gathering the information contained in this volume may be summarized in the statement that we assembled a number of trained specialists to live awhile among the Islanders and get as intimately acquainted with them as possible. Such intimacy was especially favored by three fortunate circumstances. (1) The people are less suspicious of strangers than most Negroes. They accept a visitor with hospitality and frankness, and show no hesitancy in allowing intimate views of the community in action. (2) We had the endorsement of Penn School, in whose leadership the Islanders have the utmost confidence. Without this endorsement and without the active cooperation of Misses Cooley and House, the co-principals, Mrs. King, the nurse, Miss Price, the demonstration agent, and Mr. Barnwell, the farm demonstration agent, much detail would have escaped the investigators. (3) Many facts concerning the community are matters of record. The Penn School workers have records covering the past twenty-five years, and much valuable historical material concerning the ante-bellum plantation system was uncovered in family collections. The events of the Civil War and reconstruction are matters of Government record, and interesting first-hand observations on the early days of the experiment were printed in *The Diary and Letters of Laura M. Towne* and in *Port Royal Letters*.

The chief objective of the study was to secure a picture

HOW WE GOT ACQUAINTED

of the development of the whole community rather than of some one set of habits and institutions such as are usually described in studies of health, or agriculture, or education. The approach to the whole community has the obvious advantage of relating each community activity to its whole setting, of showing its dependence upon other phases of community life. By this process we become aware of the relation of superstition to health, of education to breadwinning, of religion and crime; and we begin to glimpse the unity of the community, the tightly interwoven mesh of its structure.

To weigh the facts concerning even so simple a community as St. Helena a variety of methods were necessary. In describing the composition, characteristics and movement of the population, the census data were compiled for the township as of 1910 and 1920 and the survey staff enumerated the population as of 1928. Native enumerators were used, the same in many cases as those used by the census. These men were not as accurate as a highly trained corps, but their inaccuracies were compensated by their intimate knowledge of the neighbors whom they were enumerating. As a check on their accuracy, their work was compared name by name with the Census of 1920 and all discrepancies taken up with the enumerator for explanation. This check indicated that the Census of 1920 was probably a slight under-count, or that a large number of people were working away from home during the 1920 enumeration. It also indicated that our first enumeration was an under-count, but the check with the census and with the birth certificates supplied a full enumeration.

Only the population enumeration was complete. Almost

all the blanks gave information as to land and animals and houses, but owing to the limitations of the enumerators the income data was secured for only about half the families. This half, however, constitutes a fairly balanced sample.

The use of the historical method of interpreting origins was particularly illuminating. It is well-nigh impossible to account for such an institution as the praise house and such a custom as the shout without knowledge of the organization of the ante-bellum plantation. The manner in which the Negroes acquired their land accounts in part for their attitude toward its ownership.

The historical inquiry extended over a wider area than the Island itself. The whole Sea-Island area, from just above Charleston to just below Savannah, was more or less uniform in culture before 1860, and for this reason material from the whole area was collected. A painstaking house-to-house canvass among the descendants of former planters was richly rewarded by historical documents too valuable to be presented entirely in this brief volume. It has been separately written up in detail and will be published separately. A running summary was made in Chapter II, and in several of the chapters the past stages of an institution have been pictured from material drawn from these historical researches.

But some of the origins of the folkways of this community were too obscure to be traced in such documents as are ordinarily handled by the historian. Such origins were sought by the methods of cultural anthropology. Here chief reliance was placed upon comparison of culture traits on St. Helena with similar traits elsewhere. The origins of the peculiar dialect were traced painstakingly in English dialect dictionaries; the origins of the stories and superstitions in the folklore of other people of African descent; the origins of the spirituals in early American hymn-books. Many of these songs and stories were recorded verbatim for further analysis on the ediphone. This study of folklore also developed rich detail too voluminous for this report. It will also be published separately for reference. A running summary is given in Chapter III.

Further light on the traits of the people was gained from the measurements of psychology and physical anthropology. Much of the attention of the psychologist was centered upon the problem of securing tests appropriate to such a group—tests more or less independent of language difficulties and those not emphasizing the time factor strongly. The technical results of these tests and measurements have also been reserved for separate publication. As far as this volume is concerned they are reenforcing evidence for the conclusion that St. Helena furnishes as pure-blooded an African group as can be found for study in this country.

The study of government activity was confined to the financial aspects of the topic, because it is through the financial transactions that the attitude of the state and county to this township can be most clearly traced. The material was drawn chiefly from the county records.

The economic and sociological method, reenforced by the historical, was used in the study of the customs and organizations having to do with the population structure, the family, health, breadwinning, play, education, crime and religion. In these phases of the study the statistical method was reenforced by case studies typifying social situations. For example, the facts as to agriculture were secured from the enumeration of farm land, animals, and income. These statistics showed a group of about 85 men to be rather successful in their operation. As intimate acquaintance as possible was sought with these successful operators, in order to facilitate the accurate description of the differences between them and the general run of island farmers. Likewise the statistical analysis revealed a large proportion of old widows with adopted children, and some of these were closely observed in order that this type of family might be accurately pictured.

The general logic back of many of the conclusions follows these steps: (1) Here is a group of pure-blooded Negroes, hence next to nothing in their community life can be traced to biological relationship with the white people. (2) Here is a relatively isolated group whose earlier contacts with white culture were more frequent than the present contacts. (3) While physical isolation is pronounced, psychic contacts with white culture come through the classroom and community program of Penn School and its extension workers. Hence the adoption of modern white standards is due to this influence. (4) Other advances in culture in fields not touched by Penn School must be attributed largely to the Negroes themselves.

STATISTICAL INFORMATION

TABLE I

Total Population St. Helena Township
Censuses of 1880 to 1920 and Enumeration of 1928

	Population	Increase
1928	4,785 [1]	— 372
1920	5,157	— 1,330
1910	6,487	— 2,332
1900	8,819	1,072
1890	7,747	1,103
1880	6,644	....

[1] 4,665 enumerated, excluding white people and Penn School boarders, these were estimated.

TABLE II

St. Helena Negro Population by Plantations, 1928

Plantations	Members of Families Present on Island	Absent from Island
Corner	127	34
Saxtonville	119	19
Wallace	206	44
White Church	3	4
Fuller	100	21
Oaks	148	60
Indian Hill	75	60
Oakland	31	14
Sixty Acres	42	11
Polywanna	27	8
Datha	6	9
Wassaw	144	26
Coosaw	186	124
Mulberry Hill	14	1

Plantations	Members of Families Present on Island	Absent from Island
Hopes	82	38
Cherry Hill	16	1
Pope	6	7
John Fripp	93	34
Cedar Grove	130	65
Eddings Point	120	56
Croft	56	23
Jenkins	97	23
McTureous	54	22
Pine Grove	44	23
Coffin Point	159	103
Fripp Point	116	63
Tom Fripp	230	70
Ann Fripp	39	34
Goodman	24	14
Frogmore	214	61
Club Bridge	1	..
Pritchard	90	38
Dr. White	50	20
Cuffey	61	21
Paul Chaplin	18	18
Land's End	94	64
Tombee	88	43
Brisbane	39	13
Scott	226	62
Orange Grove	73	40
Lawrence Fripp	52	9
Oliver Fripp	43	7
Capers	162	32
Total	3,695	1,444

STATISTICAL INFORMATION

TABLE II (Con't)

Ladies Island Negro Population by Plantations

Plantations	Members of Families Present on Island	Absent from Island
Eustis	161	29
Capers	96	9
Salm Point	161	36
Woodlawn	17	3
Brickyard	50	11
Cuthbert	1	3
Hazel Farm	122	43
Bay Road	5	2
Cat Island	2	..
Unnamed	1	..
Ashdale	67	2
Johnson	26	1
Mulberry Hill	15	..
Broomfield	94	7
Fripp	70	20
Springfield	26	..
Reynolds	10	..
Robinson Village	29	..
Ferry Fisher	3	..
Maggone	4	..
Balance Ladies Island	10	..
Total	970	166
Total St. Helena plus Ladies Island	4,665	1,610

TABLE III

Population by Sections
1920 Census and 1928 Enumeration

	1920	1928	Decrease	Per Cent
Total St. Helena Township ..	4,997	4,665	332	6.6
Central Portions of the Island	2,401	2,497	96	4.0
Outlying Portions	2,596	2,168	428	16.5

TABLE IV

Sex and Age Distribution of Negro Inhabitants, St. Helena Township—Taken from 1928 Enumeration and 1910 Census

Age Group	1928				Per Cent in 1910
	Male	Female	Total	Per Cent	
0-5	144	143	287	6.2	12.5
5-10	265	286	551	12.0	15.2
10-20	626	588	1,214	26.3	27.4
20-30	313	404	717	15.5	14.3
30-40	202	295	497	10.8	9.3
40-50	241	292	533	11.6	8.1
50-60	196	240	436	9.5	6.4
60-70	124	128	252	5.5	3.8
70 and over	59	61	120	2.6	3.0
Unknown age	15	23	38		
Unknown sex and age			20		
Total	2,185	2,460	4,665	100.00	100.00

TABLE IVa

Sex and Age Distribution of Living Negro Migrants from St. Helena Township—Taken from 1928 Enumeration

Age Group	Male	Female	Total	Per Cent
0-5	11	12	23	1.5
5-10	120	153	273	17.8
10-20	339	351	690	45.1

STATISTICAL INFORMATION

Age Group	Male	Female	Total	Per Cent
20-30	185	150	335	21.9
30-40	73	71	144	9.4
40-50	22	26	48	3.1
50-60	10	5	15	.9
60-70	2	2	4	.3
70 and over				
Unknown age	42	35	77	
Unknown age and sex			1	
Total	804	805	1,610	100.0

TABLE V

St. Helena Township, Beaufort County, South Carolina
Negro Population

Negroes present in 1920 (Less Penn School Boarders)	4,997
Births	1,170
Through error or absence	599
	6,766
Migrants living (1920-1927)	1,113
Migrants dead (1920-1927)	253
Died on Island (1920-1927)	735
Total loss of population	2,101
Negroes present in 1928	4,665
Excess births over deaths (1920-1927)	435
Number of families migrated (1920-1927)	73
Number of individuals constituting family migration (1920-1927)	195
Families migrating after one or more members die (1920-1927)	26

Table VI

The gradation of migrant individuals on basis of occupations, housing, and probability of economic advancement resulted in the following distribution:

A—Very good	15
B—Good	72
C—Fair	77
D—Poor	41
E—Very bad	16
Total	221

Table VII

Negro Deaths by Age Groups, 1920-1928, St. Helena Township

Age Groups	Number of Deaths	Annual Average Deaths	Mean Population	Rate Per 1,000
0-5	86	10.8	358	30.17
5-10	21	2.6	639	4.07
10-20	60	7.5	1,292	5.80
20-30	131	16.4	714	22.96
30-40	89	11.1	510	21.76
40-50	97	12.1	514	23.53
50-60	101	12.6	423	29.79
60-70	85	10.6	250	42.40
70 and over	65	8.1	131	61.83
Total	735	91.8	4,831	19.0

STATISTICAL INFORMATION

TABLE VIII

Principal Causes of Deaths of Negroes of St. Helena Township, 1920-1928 and the Total Registration Area [1]

Cause	St. Helena Island Annual Average	Rate Per 100,000	1924 Negro Urban Registration Area Per 100,000
Heart diseases	10.75	222	291
Bowel and stomach troubles	9.87	212	[1]
Malarial fever	8.12	174	[2]
Tuberculosis	7.87	168	300
Kidney and nephritis	6.25	129	186
Old age	4.25	88	[2]
Accidents	3.62	75	114
Pneumonia	2.12	44	300
Blood troubles	2.00	41	[1]
Premature birth and other congenital causes	1.62	34	130
Pregnancy and puerperal	1.37	28	38
All other causes	36.03	750	[1]
Total	91.88	1,902	2,340

[1] The items of other deaths in the above table include an appreciable number of doubtful diagnoses as made by the undertaker since many of the deaths occurred without a physician in attendance and an annual average of twenty deaths was reported from such causes as cold and high fever. The distribution of this number to their real causes, if such could be ascertained, would undoubtedly slightly increase the rates given above for malarial fever, stomach troubles, and pneumonia.

[2] Not important cause in cities.

Table IX

Infant Mortality
(Deaths per 1,000 live births)

Rural Whites	1924	65
Rural Negroes	1924	106
Urban Whites	1924	69
Urban Negroes	1924	127
St. Helena Negroes, av. 1920-28		48

Table X

Incomes of St. Helena Families 1927 (Gross)

Under 200	130
200-300	162
300-400	164
400-500	119
500-600	58
600-700	46
700-800	39
800-900	27
900-1,000	26
1,000-2,000	24
2,000 and over	1
Total	796

STATISTICAL INFORMATION 271

TABLE XI

Size of Farms [1] of Negro Farmers of St. Helena Township

Farms	1928 No.	1925 No.	1925 Pt.	1920 No.	1920 Pt.
No. farms over 3 acres	1,201	951	100	1,119	100
Farms, by size					
Under 3 acres	75	...[2]		....[2]	
3 to 9 acres	404	332		153	
10 to 19 acres	531	384		580	
Over 20 acres	266	202		366	

[1] Data for 1920 and 1925 special tabulation of U. S. Census schedules. 1928 data from enumeration.
[2] Not enumerated as farms by the U. S. Census.

TABLE XII

Farm Land [1]

St. Helena Township

	1925	1920
All land in farms	22,784	26,168
Crop land total	10,664	17,223
Crop land harvested	6,492	14,414
Pasture land	5,271	3,356
Woodland	3,094	4,033
All other	3,755	1,556

[1] Includes both white and Negro farmers.

Table XIII[1]

Tax Levies on St. Helena Island
Fiscal Years 1921-1927

Tax levies	1921	1922	1923	1924	1925	1926	1927	Average
State levies	$4,679	$2,721	$2,138	$2,141	$1,933	$1,730	$1,709	$2,435
County levies:								
For general purposes	2,729	2,539	3,092	3,389	2,635	2,471	3,744	2,942
For schools	3,509	3,266	3,236	4,624	5,630	5,304	5,277	4,399
For roads	4,777	5,175	5,623	6,196	5,562	5,466	6,248	5,576
Total	11,015	10,980	11,951	14,209	13,827	13,241	15,219	12,917
Township or district levies:								
Beaufort-St. Helena Bridge	1,170	1,088	1,069				1,791	731
Drainage	399	363	356	357	351	330	326	354
Total	1,569	1,451	1,425	357	351	330	2,117	1,085
Grand total	$17,263	$15,152	$15,514	$16,707	$16,111	$15,301	$19,045	$16,437

[1] Source: Abstracts of the Tax Duplicates of the County of Beaufort.

TABLE XIV

Tax Levies on St. Helena Island, 1921-1927

Analyzed by Character of Tax

Year	General Property Tax			Capitation Tax			Total Tax Levies	Per Cent Total Levies in Property Taxes
	Total Taxable Property	Tax Rate Per Cent	Total Tax Levy	Number of Polls	Tax @ $4.50 Per Poll			
1921	$389,885	3.5	$13,753	780	$3,510		$17,263	79.7
1922	362,760	3.3	11,880	727	3,272		15,152	78.4
1923	356,410	3.4	12,179	741	3,335		15,514	78.5
1924	356,770	3.8	13,557	700	3,150		16,707	81.1
1925	351,370	3.9	13,703	535	2,408		16,111	85.1
1926	329,500	3.9	12,934	526	2,367		15,301	84.5
1927	325,590	5.2	16,768	506	2,277		19,045	88.0
Average	353,042	3.8	13,536	645	2,901		16,437	82.4

TABLE XV

Comparative Burdensomeness of Taxation
on St. Helena Island

Jurisdiction	Average State and Local Tax Payments		Average Income		Ratio of Taxes to Income
	Per Capita	Per Family	Per Capita	Per Family	Per Cent
St. Helena	$ 3.77 [1]	$ 16.60	$ 79 [2]	$ 420	4.00
South Carolina....	21.39 [3]	103.74	437 [4]	2,119	4.90
United States	42.69 [3]	186.55	766 [4]	3,347	5.57

[1] Average total tax collections for 1921 to 1927 inclusive as shown by tax duplicates divided by total population of Island as reported for 1920 Census.

[2] The income figures for St. Helena refer to the year 1927 and are based on individual income schedules obtained by the investigators covering over 70 per cent of the families resident on the Island.

[3] Figures refer to the year 1925 and were compiled by the National Industrial Conference Board.

[4] Figures refer to the year 1926 and were compiled by the National Bureau of Economic Research.

STATISTICAL INFORMATION 275

TABLE XVI

Estimated Value of Governmental Services of Direct Benefit to Inhabitants of St. Helena, 1921-27

Item	1927	1926	1925	1924	1923	1922	1921	Average
Road improvement [1]	$ 4,000	$ 4,000	.....	.....	.....	.....	.....	$ 1,140
Beaufort-St. Helena Bridge [2]	1,791	.....	.....	.....	.....	.....	.....	731
Education [3]	5,775 [7]	2,734	$ 3,682	$ 3,731	$ 1,069	$ 1,088	$ 1,170	3,950
Colored farm demonstrator [4]	600	600	600	600	300	300	.....	471
Drainage [5]	326	330	351	357	356	363	399	355
Outdoor poor relief [6]	190	190	190	190	190	190	190	190
Total value direct services	.....	.....	.....	.....	.....	.....	.....	6,837
Total tax levy	19,045	15,301	16,111	16,707	15,514	15,152	17,263	16,437
Per cent of taxes returned in direct services	.....	.....	.....	.....	.....	.....	.....	41.6

[1] Value of road improvement and maintenance work as estimated by a prominent white resident of the Island and by the County Road Supervisor.
[2] Amount assessed against St. Helena to meet interest and amortization charges on bridge bonds.
[3] Total school expenditures including capital outlays for St. Helena District as obtained from reports on file in the office of the State Superintendent of Education, not available back of 1924.
[4] Total appropriation for colored farm demonstrator as obtained from annual county supply bill.
[5] Total amount assessed against St. Helena District for maintenance of drainage canals.
[6] Obtained from county poor list 1927, estimated as the same in other years.
[7] Includes $2,225 for building and excludes private contributions to building.

TABLE XVII [1]

Highway Taxes Collected on St. Helena Island, 1921-27

Nature of Tax	1921	1922	1923	1924	1925	1926	1927	Average	Per Cent of Total
Property tax—county wide levy	$2,047	$2,630	$3,029	$3,746	$3,689	$3,625	$4,477	$3,320	52
Capitation road tax	2,730	2,545	2,594	2,450	1,873	1,841	1,771	2,258	36
Special district levy—bridge bonds	1,170	1,088	1,069	...	...	...	1,791	731	12
Total	$5,947	$6,263	$6,692	$6,196	$5,562	$5,466	$8,039	$6,309	100

[1] Source: Abstracts of Beaufort County tax duplicates.

STATISTICAL INFORMATION

TABLE XVIII [1]

Facts Concerning St. Helena Negro Schools, 1927-28

School	Number of Teachers	School Enrollment	Monthly Salary Roll
Lee	3	137	$125
Mulberry Hill	1	32	35
Frogmore	2	130	75
Land's End	1	76	40
South Pines	1	79	35
Oaks	1	35	35
Village	1	65	35
Eddings Point	1	78	35
Wassaw	1	56	35
Total	12	688	$445

[1] Information supplied by chairman of St. Helena School trustees. In 1928-29 there were 14 teachers with an average salary of $40 per month.

TABLE XIX [1]

Comparison of Educational Offering on St. Helena Island with Average for Beaufort County, 1927-28

	St. Helena (Negro)	Average for Beaufort County	
		White	Negro
Current expenditure per pupil enrolled [2]	$3.36	$56.00	$6.11
Length of school session in days	100	178	117
Average salary of teachers	$185	$1,004	$259
Number of pupils per teacher	57	26	46

[1] Source: Figures for St. Helena based on data obtained from State Department of Education. Figures for county obtained from 1928 Report of State Superintendent of Education.

[2] Includes expenditure for teachers' salaries, fuel and incidentals, and transportation.

Table XX[1]

Comparison of School Taxes and School Expenditure on St. Helena Island, 1924-1928

	1924-25	1925-26	1926-27	1927-28	Total
Current expense:					
White	$432	$571	$703	$1,234	$2,940
Negro	3,299	3,111	2,031	2,316	10,757
Total current expense	3,731	3,682	2,734	3,550	13,697
Capital outlays (Negro)[2]	....	....	....	2,225	2,225
Total expenditures	3,731	3,682	2,734	5,775	15,922
School taxes	4,624	5,630	5,304	5,227	20,785
Per cent of taxes taken by					
Current expense	80.7	65.4	51.5	67.9	65.9
Total expenditures	80.7	65.4	51.5	110.5	76.6

[1] Source: Reports of County Superintendent of Education to State Superintendent of Education.

[2] Includes only the proportion contributed by the county and state and excludes donations from private individuals and organizations.

Table XXI

Statistics of Penn School, 1928-29
(From Catalog)

A. Enrollment

	Girls	Boys	Men	Women	Total
Academic grades	127	137			264
Industrial (included above):					
Basketry		16			16
Blacksmithing and wheelwrighting		5			5
Carpentry		23			23
Cobbling		16			16
Cooking and housekeeping	41				41
Farm, field and orchard		36			36
Dairy and livestock		20			20

STATISTICAL INFORMATION

	Girls	Boys	Men	Women	Total
Machine repairs ...		3			3
Sewing	54				54
Gross club membership (including duplicates)	231	209	103	333	876

B. Financial

Value of plant and equipment	$155,200.00

Income:
Contributions	$ 45,640.31
School earnings	6,426.62
Interest	6,666.27
Total	$ 58,733.20

Expenditure:
Academic	$ 11,775.18
Agriculture	7,004.03
Trades	4,671.50
Boys' industries	2,259.99
Girls' industries	1,284.92
Boarding	6,041.36
Maintenance and operation	9,539.25
Administration and general	11,209.36
Extension	6,738.06
Inventory decrease	3,870.21
Total	$ 64,393.86

TABLE XXII

Number of Mothers by Number of Children Born and Living
U. S. Census of 1910

Number of Children	Mothers with Specified Number Born	Total Children Born	Mothers with Specified Number Living	Total Children Living
0	32		94	
1	89	89	174	174
2	115	230	162	324
3	78	234	147	441
4	103	412	145	580
5	103	515	129	645
6	82	492	97	582
7	71	497	71	497
8	83	684	36	288
9	63	587	36	324
10	60	600	14	140
11	62	682	13	143
12 and over	184	2,576	7	97
All families	1,125	7,598	1,125	4,235
Average		6.75		3.8

TABLE XXIII

Age and Marital Status of Heads of Households, 1928

Marital Status	Total	Ages 20-40	40-50	50-60	60-70	70 and Over
Both parents						
With children	501	143	149	102	83	24
Without children	162	69	42	16	20	15
Widows						
With children	241	31	61	55	59	38
Without children	91	16	20	17	19	19

Marital Status	Total	Ages 20-40	40-50	50-60	60-70	70 and Over
Widowers						
With children	49	5	13	15	8	8
Without children	37	3	5	10	11	8
Single						
With children	3	2	1			
Without children	50	27	13	4	3	3
Separated						
With children	10	3		4	3	
Without children	13	6	2	2	3	
Total	1,157	305	306	225	209	112

TABLE XXIV

Marital Status of Negroes, St. Helena Township 1928, Negroes in the United States 1920, Native White People in Rural Districts, 1920

Percentage of People 15 Years of Age and Over

	St. Helena Negroes	Total Negroes in the U. S.	Total Native White in the U. S.
Males	100	100	100
Single	23	33	35
Married	68	60	60
Widowed	9	6	5
Divorced and Separated	..[1]	1	..[1]
Females	100	100	100
Single	19	24	26
Married	55	60	64
Widowed	24	15	9
Divorced and Separated	2	1	..[1]

[1] Less than one per cent.

TABLE XXV

1928 Households According to Number of Rooms and Number of People

Rooms	Total	1	2	3	4	People 5	6	7	8	9	10 and over
1	26	11	4	1	3	3	..	1	2	1	
2	361	68	108	56	42	30	20	11	12	8	6
3	209	30	55	51	27	17	12	9	2	1	5
4	239	20	49	39	40	32	20	15	10	5	9
5	65	6	12	13	10	7	9	2	2	2	2
6	59	3	7	12	7	11	5	4	4	..	6
7	15	..	2	3	2	2	2	3	..	..	1
8	11	1	..	1	1	3	1	1	1	..	2
Over 8	5	..	..	2	..	1	1	..	1	..	.
Total	990	139	237	178	132	106	70	46	34	17	31

APPENDIX

Extension Work of Penn School

AMERICAN TREE ASSOCIATION.—The Tree Planting and Fire Fighting Brigade of Penn School joined the National Association in 1923. "To Plant and to Protect" is the slogan, and reports and visits to the planted trees keep up the enthusiasm.

Fruit trees have begun to take their place on the farms. This year 238 fruit trees were planted and 75 shade trees.

The tree crop on the School Farm is protected by a fire lane which serves as a continual object lesson.

ATHLETICS.—In a country day school, play should take a high rank, for country boys and girls are called upon for so much out-of-door work, play is often forgotten.

The men teachers form the Boys' Committee and the class-room teachers the Girls' Committee. The playgrounds now boast of six swings, two teeter boards, one slide, but baseball is still the most popular game with both boys and girls.

Baseball, football, basketball now take their turn; folk games and many ring games have been learned, and Penn School boys and girls have learned to play.

THE BAND.—The Penn School Band is composed of nine active members, while six boys are practising hoping to join the band at an early date. With a few leaving school each year, it means hard work and requires great enthusiasm to keep up the standard of the Penn School Band. The band is used on all community occasions, and so it helps the community as well as the morale and the pleasure of the School.

BETTER HOMES.—St. Helena Island, through the leadership of Penn School, entered the national competition in 1922. A General Committee of eight, with eight sub-committees, has carried through three successful campaigns. The first demonstration, a six-room cottage, completely furnished with borrowed furnishings, won the Third Prize. The second demonstration, a typical small island house, repaired and completely furnished with home-made furnishings, won the Second Prize. It was a "Home-made Success." And the third demonstration, the building of a house from old and new lumber, won a Special First Prize. Better homes are impossible without better homemakers, and this last "Better Home" has become our permanent practice house for 93 girls. "Better homing" has taken its place beside the better farming and the whole community used the word and the idea.

BOY'S CIVIC CLUB.—The boys of the four upper grades belong to the club. They have an executive committee of six, who with a President and Secretary-Treasurer manage the business of the club. One of the Principals is the club leader.

The aim for the year was to work for improvements in the school and home communities. A gift of $5 was made by the club to the Rosenwald School Fund.

CANNING CLUBS.—There are six clubs—and 2,450 jars of fruit and vegetables helped make Better Homes. Sew-

APPENDIX

ing, gardening, and other home interests are discussed in the meetings. The demand for more clubs is increasing.

COMMUNITY CLASS.—Those who compose this class meet every Wednesday, and as they sew on quilts which are sent to the old and needy, they sing the island spirituals. They also serve the School, for they make a strong link between the School and the community. Matters of School and community importance are discussed. The School Nurse gives them a course in home nursing, thus helping the movement for Better Homes.

CORN CLUB.—A Report from the Visiting Teacher:

"Lincoln Deas of Capers Plantation, the Winner of 1924, has been a member of the Corn Club for four years. Three successive years he failed in his work. His case was a peculiar one because his attitude toward his work in the class-room seemed all right.

"Whenever the teachers visited his acre he was very seldom seen. All of his neighbors were doing well and Lincoln was ashamed of his poor work, so he hid whenever the teachers appeared.

"But when the work for 1923-1924 began, Lincoln and his mother met the teachers at the house. He showed a new ox which was purchased the day before their arrival.

"The teachers were taken to his acre which he measured and staked off himself. Before the autumn months were over he reported his fall plowing done.

"When Planting Week came in the spring, his acre was in excellent condition. His mother bought some good seed for him and on the day appointed he dropped his seed.

"During the growing season he kept up with his crop. Once he reported that a neighbor's animal had gone into his field and eaten some of his plants, but in spite of this, the prize winner for 1924 was announced at the Farmers' Fair,—Lincoln Deas! He had the highest yield among 44 children—40 bushels and 22 quarts.

"So the boy who once stood at the foot of the chart now heads the list. His victory is one of which he himself, his School, and his teachers are proud."

CORN CLUBS.—SUMMARY FOR HOME ACRES
1917-1924

Year	Number of Pupils	Number of Acres	Acres Measured	Yield	Value
1917	138	70⅞	20½	632½	$ 948.87
1918	120	107¾	61⁷⁄₂₀	862⁷⁄₁₂	1,726.16
1919	88	54¾	27½	858¹¹⁄₁₆	1,931.04
1920	63	38¼	38¼	1,270¹⁄₁₆	1,976.27
1921	47	35½	35½	841	1,051.92
1922	(no report—crop failed)				
1923	60	32½	32½	838 Bu. 3 Qts.	838.08
1924	44	....	....	798⅞	798.86

NOTE: At the beginning of the experiment some of the younger children were included and all were on corn acres. Now that work is limited to Grades IV, V, and VI. The upper grades have a variety of projects.

DECORATION COMMITTEE.—This group has charge of the decorations needed for all community and school events.

ENTERTAINMENT COMMITTEE.—There is a monthly Community Sing; the National Week of Song is observed with a program at noon hour each day; one play party was given, and this will become a regular feature; the Christmas Mystery Play; and all other entertainments are put through by this committee.

ST. HELENA FOLK LORE SOCIETY.—Organized to preserve the folk-lore of the Islands. Through the efforts of some of its members we have secured a collection of the St. Helena spirituals. Mr. George Nicholas Julius Ballanta (Taylor), a native of Sierra Leone, East Africa, was sent down by Mr. George Foster Peabody, Chairman of our Board of Trustees, and the collection has been published. The island dialect has been preserved and the spirituals recorded by this native African whose profound interest in the songs of his people has brought forth many from the older Islanders which would have been inevitably lost had this work not been done.

GARDEN CLUB.—Gardens mean Better Homes. The club, composed of community members and boarding girls, has proved this. The garden near the Girls' Better Home, protected by a brush fence, has provided food during the winter for the cooking classes.

GIRL'S CLUB.—Once a week the girls over fourteen meet with the Principal. Topics that belong especially to girls are discussed.

GRADUATES' CLUB.—To keep the graduates in close touch with the School and to help carry the responsibility of the School is the aim of this club. A scholarship of $50 was presented to the School at its last annual meeting.

LIBRARY.—This Committee is responsible for increasing the love for reading in the community. The pupils carry the books home; lists of reading are posted in the Grades, and lists of books read are made by the pupils. Library boxes of from 30 to 40 books are sent to the county schools on St. Helena and near-by islands.

MIDWIVES' CLASS.—The first Tuesday of each month finds the midwives at Penn School, where the School Nurse gives a course of lessons prescribed by the state. Certificates are now required. Knowledge is slowly taking the place of superstition, and a higher standard is making itself felt.

Once a year Baby Day is observed, and weights and measures of the babies give the parents and midwives a concrete chart of results, and a dramatic chance to see the movement for Better Babies as it exists on the Island, the foundation of Better Homes.

POSTER COMMITTEE.—In our rural community with no local newspaper, publicity is in charge of this Committee. All public meetings are advertised by large posters, and the members are responsible for all notices sent to the churches and society meetings.

PROGRESSIVE YOUNG FARMERS' CLUB.—Twenty members grew corn and made a total yield of 503, an average of 26 bushels to the acre; while the highest yield was 43 bushels. Four of the members are also raising pigs.

POULTRY CLUB.—"The Scrubs Must Go" is the slogan of this new club. More than 530 chickens have started straight for an autumn market, and the monthly meetings have had an attendance of 100 per cent.

PUBLIC HEALTH.—Over 500 patients were cared for by the School Nurse, and preventive work was carried on among the Penn School children through the monthly weighing and measuring and the daily hot school lunch. A physical inspection was given and the parents notified of physical defects—75 defects were discovered.

The Island is most grateful to the Marine Hospital on Parris Island for its generous help in emergencies. We are also grateful for the help given by the Public Health Nurse of Beaufort County, Miss Davis, and to Dr. T. R. Meyer, the County Health Officer, who have assisted in this work.

The St. Helena physician, Dr. York W. Bailey, a Penn

School graduate, can always be counted upon for complete cooperation.

PUBLIC SERVICE COMMITTEE.—A group of pupils from the High School, elected by the pupils in the four upper grades, are responsible for the school morale. A Committee of Teachers guides them. To be a member of this Committee is the highest honor in the school.

A word for each month is chosen and posted in each class-room—Honesty, Reverence, Self-control, Self-respect, Faithfulness, Thrift, Courtesy, Gratitude, etc., all have their place. Each grade in turn presents a play on one word, two members of the Public Service Committee appearing in each play.

The members assist on the playgrounds, on the roads to and from home, while the girls assist at the daily school lunches, and the boys care for the water trough by the roadside.

THE ST. HELENA QUARTET.—The Quartet has done much to preserve the island spirituals. They are continually discovering "new ones," which means that they are finding very old ones which the younger generation have lost track of and thus might easily be lost forever.

The Quartet gave invaluable aid to Mr. Ballanta (Taylor) when he was recording the St. Helena Island spirituals.

The spirit of reverence with which the Quartet sings these songs is felt by all, and no school or community program is complete without the Quartet.

REFRESHMENT COMMITTEE.—A Committee stands ready to manage the question of refreshments throughout the year —a very important detail in a Country Community. The teacher in charge of the Home Economics is Chairman of this Committee, so the work is centralized.

SALES HOUSE.—A place where donations of barrels and packages of clothing, etc., are sent and where many a family can secure the necessities to help them keep their boys and girls in school. Here, too, the old people can get many a comfort. Prices vary according to the need; but all pay something, except the "afflicted"—and those for whom the exception must be made. Work and farm products are accepted in payment as well as cash.

ST. HELENA CREDIT UNION AND COOPERATIVE SOCIETY. —The business of the Cooperative Society is carried on by a Committee of Management of nine members, elected by the Society. Its purpose is to lend the farmers money at a reasonable rate of interest and to teach them business methods. The minimum loan has been $10 and the maximum $100.

The Society also does cooperative buying of seed and fertilizer, and cooperative marketing.

The borrowing and loaning activities of the Cooperative Society were transferred to the St. Helena Credit Union in 1924. To make possible the advanced step of share-holding by its members, according to law, each member must hold one share ($5 par value). At the annual meeting of the Cooperative Society the members voted to move into the Credit Union as a body. Thus the St. Helena farmer will save money and make his own money work for himself.

SUNDAY SCHOOLS.—Penn School has always cooperated with the local churches. Church and School go hand in hand. A daily chapel service at noon brings together the large day school family; a daily service after supper brings together the smaller boarding school family, while a Sunday evening service adds to the spiritual life. But our connection with the island churches and Sunday schools is of greatest value, and only through this connection can the "young race" learn how to carry on in their own communities.

Our teachers serve as teachers and officers, and our pupils compose the larger portion of the Sunday school scholars.

THE YOUNG MEN'S CHRISTIAN ASSOCIATION.—This plays a most important part in the making of our boys. Two meetings are held every week, so the different groups may attend. Home problems and clean living are discussed and the "Y" boys are called upon to give special service for the very old people upon emergency.

This year representatives were sent to the Association Conference held at Voorhees School in Denmark, S. C., and this experience gave a splendid impetus to their association.

THE YOUNG WOMEN'S CHRISTIAN ASSOCIATION.—This is an active organization, not only training the girls for their own religious life, but developing among them the desire for service. This year the girls helped 13 needy people; made one bed-quilt; made over three dresses for children; contributed $5 for the Rosenwald School, and subscribed $10 for the National Y.W.C.A.

—From 1925 Year Book of Penn School.